BIRTH OF A TUMBLEWEED

Memoirs of Growing Up in Post-Nazi Germany

By

Inge Perreault

This book is a work of fiction. Places, events, and situations in this story are purely fictional. Any resemblance to actual persons, living or dead, is coincidental.

ISBN: 1-4033-1169-2 (e-book)
ISBN: 1-4033-1170-6 (Paperback)
ISBN: 1-4033-1171-4 (Dustjacket)

This book is printed on acid free paper.

1st Books - rev. 08/10/02

Due to the very personal nature of this material the author has chosen to self-edit the book.

She would like to express her extreme gratitude to the following individuals who helped her proof-read the material and corrected errors.

Thank you   Fred Snowflack
            Carol Feller
            Timothy Carleton
            Gine Lombardo
            Roland Perreault
            Wayne Thorpe

and my humblest apology to those of you, who nevertheless find my errors. Kindly keep in mind that writing is an art and not a science, that an author has the right to sometimes change the rules, and last but not the least that nobody is perfect.

Dedications:

This book is dedicated to my dearest friend

Carole Cohen

Our friendship has been an enduring one for more than three decades. It has proven that love and understanding are stronger than cultural differences. Thank you Carole for encouraging me to write this book.

I would also like to express my special gratitude to Dr. Gary Safier

It is true that each person, each segment of society, and each individual country or part of the world has a lifestyle and culture, which are uniquely its own; yet, when the surface is scratched and the depth of character is allowed to shine, it is revealed that the light of each person, each segment of society, and each individual country or part of the world has the same glow. It is the glow of humanity.

The ability to celebrate the differences while, at the same time, coaxing out the humanity is the theme of Inge's story and the theme of Inge's life.

Carol Cohen-Hyde

This story is written for all people, whose suffering due to war has been forgotten, since quite innocently they may have found themselves on the wrong side of a historical conflict. It is representative of the suffering and the collective guilt placed on innocent victims of circumstances beyond their control, as well as that of their descendents.

It is not the intention of the writer to diminish the indescribable horror of the Holocaust, but tells the story of millions of people, whose suffering history has chosen to ignore.

While this is my story, I am writing it not only as a personal catharsis but for all people, irrespective of color, race or religion who have, or are at present, on the wrong side of a political conflict and are thus expected to survive, endure and heal without having a voice.

Thus I decided to speak for them all!

The Early Years

Memories of my childhood seem to go back further than those of most people I know. True, they are somewhat fuzzy about the early days, especially when I was still a baby in diapers and drinking from a bottle, but nevertheless they are there.

I can still picture in my mind the old brick apartment house on the outskirts of Cologne, where my family took refuge after the war. The city, where my mother grew up, had been reduced to a pile of rubble from the unrelenting and prolonged bombing attacks by the allied forces. From my mother I would later be told often about the once beautiful ancient city, dominated by the largest Gothic Cathedral in the world, 800 years under construction. A city, founded by the Romans under Nero's mother Queen Colonia Aggripina 2000 years ago and separated by the

1

Rhine river, with beautiful old buildings hundreds of years old, now turned into the nightmare of the skeletal remains, unrecognizable to those who had been happy living here. Rhinelanders were renowned for being light-hearted and fun-loving people. Now the survivors stood devastated in mind and spirit in the midst of ruins which once had been their homes, hardly comprehending how all this could have happened.

I remember cramped quarters, since there were my grandparents, both already past 80, my two sisters, 12 and 9 years older than me, my father and my mother living in two rooms. Three things stand out sharply in my mind: sitting by the window on my beloved grandmother's lap, who never tired of reading fairy stories to me, the small backyard with the crude sandbox and the little farmer's daughter across the street, proud owner of a wooden rocking horse I was allowed to ride on rare occasions. To this day I have a great fondness for old-fashioned rocking horses. I would have loved to own one myself when I was little, and I made sure my sons grew up with the pleasure I was deprived of.

There are other memories, but I have never been able to place them in the proper order and it really does not matter, since I know the events all had to have taken place prior to my third birthday. Sometime during my second year of life we moved further out into the country. My father purchased a good-sized piece of property in the midst of fields on a dirt path with no name, on which he and my grandfather at first built a basement with a one-room wooden shack. At least now we were able to grow all of our own food. But that definitely occurred sometime prior to my turning three. Before that, there are memories of my sisters having to take me along in my carriage much against their will and leaving me down by the Rhine-river meadows while they played with their friends. I remember taking some minor abuse from my sisters who, as I was to find out soon enough, were half sisters. My mother's husband had died early on in the war on the Russian front at age 28, leaving her to fend for herself, two small children and aging parents, through one of the worst periods of the twentieth century.

My sisters discovered that pinching their baby sister's cheeks they could make me cry, and when out of my mother's or grandmother's sight, would amuse themselves as children often do, by alternatively pinching and kissing me. This fact alone left me in a very confused state of mind but had ultimately proven a good lesson in life. They did not mean any harm, since I was later told that when crying I had the most adorable facial expression, but as I now reflect on these occurrences at the age of 54, experience has shown me, that oftentimes the people we love most will inflict the greatest pain.

At the time the muddy river seemed huge and frightening. Thus I sat quietly in my old rickety carriage sucking on my pacifier, while watching the other children play.

The particular odor of the wide river is another memory deeply embedded in my mind.

If I close my eyes I can still conjure up the distinct somewhat musty smell to this very day. At this particular point the Rhine curves sharply and is extremely wide. To a very small child it seemed like a huge monster, flowing along slowly the color of mud and riverbanks lined with scraggly trees, bearing the signs of being flooded on a regular basis.

In the fall they looked like ghosts to me, reaching out to grab me and pull me into the muddy waters.

Now that I have opened the Pandora's box, memories come flooding back to me and I vividly recall my dear grandmother, a tiny woman with long gray hair tied into a neat bun, who always dressed in a long black frock. One morning grandmother faints right by my side on the cobblestone pavement, while we are waiting for the milkman. I can still hear the porcelain milkjug shattering into a thousand pieces and feel the fright and utter helplessness of seeing my "Oma" lying unconsciously on the sidewalk.

Actually, at this point, my grandmother forms the centerpiece of my life, more so than my mother, always too busy trying to feed the family. My sisters have to go out and ask the farmers for permission to go over the harvested grain and potato fields to pick up the leftovers. The grain goes into the old coffee grinder and provides a coarse flower for bread or pancakes, and many buckets of potatoes missed by the harvesting equipment are salvaged from the potato fields. The farmers are wealthy these days. They have more than enough to eat and drive a hard bargain. I hear that some of them have so many valuable oriental rugs, that they are stacked in rolls in the barns. People will trade in their most treasured possessions just to have food to eat. The basic staples, such as flower, potatoes and eggs carry a high price, since the rationing coupons just do not make end's meet.

One day Mama has a terrible argument and screaming match in the hallway with her older sister Anna, who also lives in the same apartment house. They fight fiercely over a two-piece kitchen hutch, which my aunt and her husband are carrying out of our apartment, claiming it to be theirs. But Mama is no fool; they get away with the top piece but the bottom piece stays and I remember it for a long time. Eventually my father finds another top and paints it a matching color. While the argument is in full swing I am pressing myself into the corner of the hallway, clinging to Mama's skirt while crying bitterly. I am afraid!

Memories are so very strange. The multitude of things we remember as adults at times seem rather insignificant, however to a child of such a tender age they are simply monumental. Thus I even recall being scolded for wetting my pants while playing in the sandbox, the most scratchy and uncomfortable hand-knitted woolen underpants ever made. I also remember well the very evening I throw up the milk I drink from my bottle and my subsequent refusal from then on to touch milk ever again. Just the smell of it to this day brings back the nausea I experienced.

5

Then there is the unpleasant event of Tante Grete, my favorite aunt, taking me to the doctor, since running about barefoot I got a splinter lodged deep under my toenail. The doctor puts me to sleep with ether while my toenail is cut open and the splinter removed.

There is still a ridge in the middle of the nail of my big toe attesting to the validity of this event. On the way home I get rather sick to my stomach several times and have to vomit by the fence of a field, where a chestnut-colored horse is grazing. I like that horse. Just watching it, as well as the tall fragrant grass and colorful field flowers make me feel better.

One memory that haunts me for the rest of my life is my inability to go to sleep unless someone holds on to my little hand. This chore is normally given to one of my step-sisters. They hate it and try to sneak away at the first sign of my falling asleep, at which point I awaken immediately and start to cry. Somehow, deep down in the very core of my little being, is this inexplicable sense of anxiety and fear of abandonment. Where did that come from, I wonder? Is it possible that being born so shortly after the war I somehow shared in my mother's exhaustion and misery, being influenced adversely in the very womb which gave me life?

Times are so very difficult and a child as perceptive as I am, picks up easily on past and present stresses and uncertainties. All I know is that anxiety is my constant unwelcome companion and that's why I use a pacifier until the age of almost six. It has become my "security blanket."

I do not see too much of my father during those early years since he is always working, and if not working he is looking for means to feed the family. Because he had been a soldier during the war, he was sentenced by the Allied Forces, in this case Cologne being under British rule, to ten

6

years of hard labor for minimum wage at a local glass factory. Prior to the war he had no choice in joining the party if he wanted to keep his job with the railroad, which he needed to support a wife and 3 young children.

That had been the cause of many arguments in his family, since my paternal grandfather, a binge-drinker and stern man who inflicted many wounds on his wife and children, physical as well as mental, had been a staunch communist when Hitler took power.

But again, my father did what he had to, in order to keep his job and put food on the table. Germany had just come out of the Great Depression and the period of hyperinflation when, if you were lucky enough to have a job, at the end of the day you were handed a suitcase full of money and rushed to the local bakery, in the hope you might be able to purchase a single loaf of bread with your trillions of banknotes. If you were not, you might just as well go ahead and burn the entire lot, since you knew it would be worthless by morning!

Working the glass ovens Papa says is hot, dirty and exhausting shift labor. He does not like it at all. Consequently I see little of him, although when I do, he is always very loving and kind. Much later I find out that my father, just on a rumor, takes a six hour train ride in an open transport car during the midst of winter all the way to Hanover, but returns triumphantly with a sack of potatoes.

Somehow through barter, ingenuity and thrift my family does not go hungry but survives on what can be bought with rationing coupons or be acquired by the above mentioned means.

The actual move to the country is one of those fuzzy parts of my memory during the early years. All I remember is that one day, all of our meager belongings are loaded into a wooden, hand-drawn wagon pulled by my father and grandfather, and we move into the one-room shack, where all of us sleep on the floor the first few nights. I cannot even remember what time of year it is. During the following months the shack is added onto and eventually consists of 3 rooms, heated by a coal stove in the kitchen and one in the living room. It is not pretty! From the outside it is covered with tarpaper but inside it is cozy and spotlessly clean. Papa has made the windows himself, using flawed discarded glass containing little air bubbles from the glass factory where he has to work. There are handmade shutters which are closed nightly to keep out the winter cold and rain, so frequent in this part of Germany. There is no electricity. Light is provided at night by means of an old-fashioned oil lamp. I must be three years old by now.

Oftentimes, all of us sit in the dark by the glow of the burning coals in the stove to save precious lamp oil. Those are nights that I partially cherish, because there are chestnuts roasting on top of the stove or apples baking in the oven.

Unfortunately, more often than I like, those evenings are also haunting, because I have to listen over and over to troublesome stories about the big war that frighten me so. I hear about the endless nights Mama, my sisters and grandparents had spent in the basement of their brownstone in Cologne, being bombed nightly for two long years.

My sisters had started screaming hysterically when the warning sirens had gone off and the air raids started. I sit on Oma's lap and hold on to her real tight when they talk about these events.

One night, the occupant of the next brownstone, a prominent physician whose basement had been fortified, asked Opa to spend the night with him and his family since he felt his place to be safer. My grandfather graciously declined. A sense of premonition seems to run in my family for I certainly have it. That very night the doctor's house had taken a direct hit by a bomb, killing everyone who sought refuge there. The force of the blast had been so strong that it had thrown all members of my family against the far end of the basement wall, where they had lain on the ground dazed for quite some time. Although this occurred prior to my being born, in my imagination I can see clearly every detail and that is very scary. Many years later I find out that after the war Mama had gone back and had dug in the rubble with her hands to find something, anything, to remind her that she once lived there. All that had been left in one piece had been a porcelain soup tureen and a metal cookie container.

Likewise, the trip of the evacuation to Poland by horse-drawn wagon in the midst of winter, during which my family had witnessed some horrific sights, such as traitors

9

hanging from lamp posts and more hardships than my little mind can comprehend, causes me to have nightmares. By then my mother's first husband had died on the Russian front. He had only been 28 years old and in his last letter my mother ever received he had written, that he was able to see the towers of St. Basil's Cathedral in Moscow from the distance. Shortly thereafter, while in the hospital with a concussion because a brick had fallen on Mama's head, the family had received the rather matter-of-fact notification that her husband, the father of her two little girls, had proudly given his life for the Fuehrer. What cold-blooded foolishness I think, remembering my mother talking about the pain she had felt. I know that my mother's first husband had never believed in the government, had never wanted to go to war but had been drafted. I know what he looked like because Mama keeps a framed photograph of him with his death notice and a little heart-shaped vase with dried flowers in her bedroom. His name was Hans. He was a good man with Coke-bottle-thick, dark-rimmed glasses due to poor eyesight and had his own business as a tile roofer. According to Mama, after the occurrence of "Kristallnacht," he had placed his head on the table in disgust, then looked up at her with sad eyes and said: "Agnes, this will not end well." As history records he had been absolutely correct and it had cost him his young life.

In Poland my Mama met Papa and she, being a young and very beautiful widow, had captured the heart of my father, a married man from Saxony in the eastern part of Germany. Since he had been an extremely shy youngster, he had allowed himself during the depression to be talked into a loveless marriage by his own mother. The marriage nevertheless had produced three children, one son and two daughters. In Poland, he had fallen hopelessly in love with my attractive and vivacious mother, a "Rhinelander," which he eventually would pay for with the bitter price of my mother's unmet expectations, scorn and never ending arguments.

Papa's stories of the big war which are told on those memorable nights are also very frightening and gruesome. He had been drafted along with all of his 5 brothers, and he tells us how his superior at the railroad where he was employed, had called for him one day with a proposal. It had been strongly suggested to him that there was a "cushy" job with little danger available. After all, was he not a married man with three young children? The position had been that of a guard at the "work camp" Bergen Belsen. By that time Papa had heard rumors, and since he was an extremely sensitive person, he had firmly declined answering: "I cannot execute such duty, I am sorry but please assign me to another position." He also would never forget the local Jewish tailor who, when he had been just a little boy, treated him very kindly in providing a little suit and cap for him free of charge. His strict father, a mason by trade, had only been able to afford new suits for his two older brothers, leaving Papa with "hand-me-downs." But the tailor had always insisted that the little one likewise needed a new suit. He subsequently had fashioned one from leftover material, much to my father's delight. Now the tailor and his family were missing!

Papa's superior had become extremely angry and had asked him if he would like to go to Bergen Belsen as an inmate? However, my Papa had stood his ground and repeated that he could not take the position, no matter what!

Subsequently, he had been given one of the most dangerous duties, other than being assigned to the front lines. He had been put in charge of taking trains loaded with supplies to the Russian front. Naturally, the trains had been a constant target for bombing attacks. I remember the story about the time in Smolensk, where they had stopped for the night. Next to them, there had been a train full of wounded German soldiers in transport back to Germany from the Russian front. Papa and his friends had sat in the caboose of their train that night playing cards, when suddenly the tell-tale sound of approaching Russian planes had made them leave the train and run away from the station as fast as their legs could carry them. Papa had thrown himself into the nearest ditch, and when the fury of the fiery attack had passed, he had checked whether he still had all his limbs.

Then, to his horror, he had detected an unexploded grenade that had gone into the ground no further than five inches from his head. Right there, in that ditch, he had fallen to his knees and had thanked God for sparing his life. When he had returned to the station, the sight he had found was one of utter chaos and terror. The train cars had resembled colanders full of holes and the station platform had been covered with dead bodies as well as severed limbs. Wounded soldiers from the other train had dragged themselves behind the huge steel wheels of the train but the grenades had pierced the steel and killed them anyway. As long as my father was alive, he never forgot the sight of a single finger wearing a wedding band, as well as the stench of burned human flesh. It haunted him for the rest of his existence here on earth and he spoke to me about it often. He had vomited, cursed, cried tears of desperation and fury at the senselessness. Then he had pulled himself together with the few survivors of this fierce attack, only to be put in charge of another train, transporting supplies to the front lines.

When those had broken during the harsh Russian winter and the Russian tanks had been closing in on them, it had been every man for himself. He literally had run for his life. Two events he told leave indelible impressions on me. Once, when Papa had been near total exhaustion, he had come to a remote Russian farmhouse, where an old Russian woman had treated him very kindly. Finding him collapsed on a pile of hay in the barn, she had brought the frightened young man a large jug of fresh milk, still warm from the cow, and urged him to drink. Then she had sent him on his way with her blessings, for she too was a mother with a son at the front lines, hoping that her son might encounter equal treatment from a compassionate soul, even though they fought on different sides.

The other event still makes me sad. Papa had been a good runner and on the flight from the Russians a fat man, who could not move as fast, had begged him to wait, had even promised him cartons of cigarettes. But Papa never smoked and he had known that he simply had no time to wait. He had been running for his life! Consequently, in my mind I see this poor fat man loosing ground, being all alone and terrified, most likely brutally killed by the Russians. I have a tender heart and I still feel very sorry for this unfortunate human being. While I understand my father's point, I like to think I would have waited and not left this poor man all alone to meet a terrible fate.

In Poland, where his regiment had regrouped, my father had clearly realized that the war was lost and distributed the supplies he had been in charge of to the Polish civilians.

This kind act had nearly cost him his life. One of his superiors had found out and marked him as a traitor. It had been my mother who had heard about the danger my father had found himself in. She herself had gone and pleaded with the official on her knees, begging him not to send the fateful letter to the authorities, for otherwise my father's life would surely have ended with a shot to the head.

Ultimately my father took great pride in the fact that he made it through the entire second World War without ever firing his gun. He had encountered Hitler once, up close, when the Fuehrer had come to inspect the troops. Funny enough, he had stopped right in front of Papa and had looked him straight in the eye. My father had looked straight back at him and later said that he had never in his life seen such scary eyes, black bottomless pits like those of a shark, devoid of any emotion. The man had truly frightened him!

There were other things he told about which were not confirmed until decades later and, to my knowledge, most history books neglect to mention them even today. At the beginning of the war, when the German Army marched into Poland, many a German soldier had been found hanging on meat hooks, the work of Polish terrorists. At one point my father and his fellow soldiers had come upon a strange looking part of a forest, named the Forest of Kathuen, where they had found a very large disturbed area, freshly replanted with young birch trees. Their commander had ordered them to dig up part of the area where they had made a very gruesome discovery. Here they had found Stalin's work, mass graves were containing the remains of the Polish Aristocracy and intelligentsia, many of them Jewish. But history books do not mention those horrors and I wonder why?

On other nights my mother tries to cleanse herself and regain some sort of peace of mind by telling stories of her own wartime experiences. She tells how they had fled from Poland back to Germany, again by horse-drawn wagon, much like the pictures she witnesses in the 90s of refugees in the Balkans. Even then, so many years later, she would experience extreme anxiety and had to leave the room or shut the TV off.

Hearing the roar of approaching Russian tanks and distant artillery, the endless stream of wagons, once again in the midst of a brutally cold winter, had passed a walking column of people guarded by German soldiers. Mama had asked a soldier who these people were and had received the grumpy answer that these were merely Jews and the entire matter none of her concern. At one point a young girl had left the line and begged Mama to take her in. The soldier had walked over, hit the pretty girl over the head with the butt of his rifle, ordering her back into line. Mama had become very angry and had yelled at the German soldier, who had then pointed his rifle straight at her asking, if she wished to exchange places with the girl. Naturally, my mother, with two small children and elderly parents to care for, had been forced to think about her own family. But she would never forget this senseless brutality. To her great pleasure she had noticed later on, that an elderly couple traveling alone had allowed the young girl to slip into their covered wagon unseen.

The journey back had been filled with bitter cold, sickness, hunger and especially fear, for the Russian army was approaching fast. Rumors of every woman in sight being raped and brutally murdered spread like wildfire and later proved to be correct.

Even pregnant women, very young girls or grandmothers had not been spared.

From Poland Papa had been dispatched to Norway, where he had spent a year. Had it not been for having fallen in love with my mother, he would not have returned from

15

there. He had loved the country, as well as the people. Longingly he would in later years talk of the beautiful town of Oslo, the magnificent mountains, fjords and deep forests. He had been sent as far as Hammerfest, where in the summer you could grow the most gorgeous vegetables within a few weeks time, since it was so close to the Arctic Circle that the sun never set. Papa always had been a great gardener. This period of the war in Norway had been a peaceful time for him.

When the war was finally lost and his platoon shipped back to Bremen, he and his best friend had gotten rid of their uniforms and sworn to each other never to disclose to anyone, which branch of the army they had been part of. This had proven to be a smart move, because upon landing in Bremen they had been met by American troops and walking down the plank of the boat they had been kicked and beaten. Some soldiers had been shot right then and there because they had belonged to the most despised part of the armed forces, the Waffen SS. Papa and his friend had made the right decision and had been sent to a prison camp outside Hamburg. There they had spent miserable winter months in an open field. Many soldiers, weakened from the war, had died from pneumonia and dysentery. Then, one day, they had simply been released and free to go. Somehow Papa had made his way to Cologne looking for Mama.

It is still a mystery to me how he ever managed to find her.

He did not want to return to his first wife and children in what had now become East Germany under Russian control. The Russian Army took revenge on the Germans. Thus, this again had been a wise decision, since it was not until the Berlin Wall fell in 1990, that the full extent of

16

what the Russian troops had done was discovered in the form of huge mass graves containing the remains of Germans. While he provided for his family back East with what little he had until his three children finished University, he himself only returned once for the burial of my grandfather. He did not even stay the night but took the next train back to West Germany. The communist regime had made him feel very uneasy.

My paternal grandmother had passed away at the end of the war after having been buried for days under the debris of her home, which had been hit by a Russian bomb on the very last day of the war. Papa had also lost a younger brother, shot in the back by Serb terrorists, as well as his favorite 12 year old nephew, who had been buried alive with his mother but died before he could be reached.

All the above and more is enough to cause me many sleepless nights. In my innocence I do not understand that everyone in my family is suffering acutely from post-traumatic stress and needs ways to cope with their experiences.

I should never have heard what I hear at my age, but my parents are ignorant of the psychological effect it will have on a little girl like me. The scars they inflict unintentionally can never be erased.

Thus, I have rather ambiguous feelings about those nights spent in front of the coal-burning stove, for they provide both: togetherness and fear. Life is hard for all of us after the war, but at least there is peace now.

For a little girl my age, I am close to four by now, some of the inconveniences matter little. I simply do not know any better. For instance there is no running water.

Papa somehow obtains a big tank, and every day Mama and grandfather pull it on the old wooden wagon to the nearest house, at least a mile or so away, to get water.

There is an outhouse and in the summertime refrigeration consists of a large earthenware crock, dug into a shady area near the homestead, where the perishables are kept. A bath is taken once a week on Saturday nights in a big tin tub, when my long blond hair is washed.

Since I am the youngest I always end up with the water in which my older sisters bathed before me, a fact I tolerate without complaining but do not like at all.

The piece of property is large and seems endless to me, since it is located in the midst of wheat fields. On a clear day I can even see the spires of the Cologne Cathedral. A narrow dirt path leads to the pine forest not too far away as well as another one to the nearest village with a store. For my amusement Papa builds me a big swing made of simple boards near the end of the property, where I spend many lonely hours dreaming of playmates and contemplate life in general.

My father rides his old bicycle to work and my sisters ride theirs to school, leaving me alone in the company of Mama and my grandparents for much of the time. While I like growing up in the fields, having chickens, ducks and a cat, I miss the company of other children my own age. Of my sisters I remember little. As a matter of fact, I cannot even remember what my oldest half-sister used to look like then. She has been sent to a convent teaching the nursing profession but refuses to stay there after a year since she is a fun-loving young girl and does not like the strict rules of the nuns. I can recall the face of my second older half-sister and her brown hair in long braids.

At this point neither of them bother much with their little sister. They have friends in school and there is such a large age difference between us.

One of my major sources of dissatisfaction, even at age 4, is the fact that I do not have my own bed. Since Papa works shift-work I am allowed to sleep in his bed one week, the other days I am shuffled about. This fact bothers me a lot and contributes to my inability to fall asleep at night, as well as creating a feeling of not belonging.

Looking back, I try hard to concentrate on the joyous moments of my early childhood, because already at the tender age of 4 I have made up my mind that this is not my home.

Wistfully, I look up into the sky where the clouds always seem to be hanging much too low, and it is then that the TUMBLEWEED longing and part of my character slowly begin to take shape.

The good times are those I spend in the company of my Oma and Opa (grandparents).

Just like yesterday I remember these two wonderful old people, always dressed in black, faithfully taking an afternoon walk every day into the woods, where among others they collect pinecones to start the morning fires in the stove. It is my greatest joy being allowed to accompany them, for they teach me many things about plant and animal life.

Walking between them, holding my grandmother's hand on one side and my grandfather's on the other, I feel grounded. I belong and remember resting with them, sitting on a fallen tree log, while being loved and adored. How could these two old people, well into their eighties, have coped, had it not been for me and the promise of a new beginning; a renewal of hope after a lifetime that saw three wars. While life had been hard for them during the first two, the third one had robbed them of everything, their house blown into a pile of rubble and all that is left now are the clothes on their backs and a little girl, to whom they can give all their love and affection. Since I am born out of wedlock they even give me their last name, and to this very day I proudly display a framed copy of their Coat of Arms dating back to 1735, when the name "Windelschmidt" meant weapon smith and was attached to a prestigious heritage and profession.

Yes, those are truly magic times. I learn about flowers and nature in general, but also the harsh reality of having to circumvent foxholes left over from the war with a stern admonition, to never venture out into the woods by myself, since unexploded bombs, grenades and landmines pose an ever-present danger. The knowledge of that and hearing what happened to other children while innocently playing, are enough of a deterrent for me to be scared and thus obey the strict rule. These aftereffects of a war are so hard to comprehend and digest, especially for a small child like me.

My mind skips several decades ahead, and I recall a visit to my then elderly parents in 1990, when I take the bus to Cologne which passes right by my former high school.

There is an extensive detour. When I question one of the fellow passengers he informs me that, while laying a new gas line, workers have come across a large unexploded bomb from the war, approximately six feet below the road surface. This was the very road I took to school on my bicycle for years, totally unaware of the danger which lurked beneath. It causes a chill to run down my back and instant anxiety.

Americans of my husband's generation cannot identify with the feelings such occurrences cause to well up in me. I remember well my husband's facial expression of astonishment, when on our honeymoon returning from New York to my parents' home, we visit the old part of Cologne and he notices bullet holes in some of the old houses.

I imagine only the American people who lived through the civil war could have identified with what it was like to grow up in a country so totally devastated. Plus there is the underlying feeling abroad I will experience many times, that after all the Germans got what they deserved. The fact that innocent people suffered, history chooses to ignore completely. The same has happened to millions of people since all over the world. Realistically seen it will continue to happen. Finally, past 50 years of age, I have resigned myself to that sad fact.

One of the very best memories of those days is that of my grandfather taking me to the town where he had grown up, the son of a wealthy owner of a lumberyard.

There we share our meager lunch on the outskirts of town, in the woods by the side of a merry little waterfall. Just Opa and me, sitting on the rocks watching the water bugs scoot across the quiet pool into which the little stream collects. We talk about a lot of things and he answers patiently all of his little granddaughter's curious questions.

I fondly remember it as one of the highlights of my entire life, for the love we share that day will remain in the recesses of my heart forever.

Opa is very concerned about us children. From his small pension he saves up money to buy a beautiful fountain pen for my sister's birthday. While I do not have any recollection of early Christmas celebrations, I do remember Opa and Oma taking me out for an Easter walk into the woods, where I find colorful eggs hidden by the side of tree stumps and in the green moss along a little stream, wondering how the Easter Bunny could have known we were going to pass by. It takes a few more years for me to figure out who the illusive Easter Bunny is. Opa is determined for us children to enjoy life and so that particular Easter he also surprises me with a Max und Moritz book by Wilhelm Busch, a classic for little children with cartoon figures telling the story of two naughty little boys.

Spring is very nice that particular year. It is just prior to my fifth birthday, and I watch the farmer next to our property plow the fields around me with his enormously big and strong Belgian draft horse. He walks slowly behind the plough while the animal pulls with all its might. I just love the smell of the freshly turned earth, there is something very special about it. One day the young farmer picks me up, when he notices the little girl who is watching him intently. Gently he places me on the back of the huge animal. My legs stick straight out from either side, since the back of the horse is so wide. He laughs and jokes with me, and from then on we become friends: the farmer, the horse and the little girl with the long, blond wavy hair. I am a curious child, always asking questions about what he is planting, when it will ripen as well as endless questions about the huge but gentle animal which is his companion.

In June, when the wheat is as high as my head, I can be seen picking brilliant red poppies and bright blue cornflowers which grow in profusion among the grains. Prior to pesticides and herbicides any field of wheat, rye or barley is a canvass of color, unmatched by any painter in its natural beauty. Once the grain is ready to be harvested and has turned a golden yellow the farmer returns, cuts it and stacks it to dry in the shape of an Indian tent. I take the only two toys I own, an old doll named Marlene with a large crack along her back and a pink teddy bear, a gift from my grandfather, and play house inside the "grain-tents."

Sometimes I return home with bloody feet, since the grain stubble turns hard and sharp cutting my bare feet, but it still provides a great playtime. The only thing which would make it more enjoyable would be a companion, but that is not to be for another year. So I am left to my own vivid imagination.

Once my mother takes me to a nursery school in the next village that is run by Carmelite Catholic Nuns. Their big white headdress scares me. Even though there are a lot of other children and wonderful toys, I cry the entire time and finally find a place for myself in the shade of a large tree. There I observe from afar, while waiting desperately for Mama's return.

The variety of food begins to be more plentiful since we grow just about every type of vegetable and have our own chickens. So far sugar beet syrup which is inexpensive and plentiful in our area, since sugar beets grow well in sandy soil, has been used often instead of jam on slices of rye bread. All of us have grown tired of the taste by now, and so one day we have a special event I shall never forget. Papa has been buying sugar beet syrup by the bucket since it does not need refrigeration. That day my sisters are asked to dig a hole in the backyard and all of us, including my grandparents, assemble and almost ceremoniously empty the last bucket of syrup, watching it quietly seep into the ground. It is not a celebration because not a word is spoken, yet in a strange way it actually is and all of us know that. We are past the worst! We made it and though somehow the act seems wasteful, there is a lot of symbolism attached to this family event.

Late that autumn I catch the measles and lie on the sofa of the living room under an open umbrella to shield me from the light of the oil lamp, by which my sisters do their homework. I am utterly miserable for weeks and the doctor is summoned for several visits. When I finally recover winter has arrived with unusually cold temperatures and a lot of snow, so that the glass panes of the windows are covered completely with lovely ice flowers. I imagine that is what the castle windows in the fairy story the Snow Queen must look like. I scratch away some of the ice with my fingernails in order to peek outside. It turns out to be a very long winter. Due to my weakened condition I am not allowed outside and there is so little to play with. I long for building blocks. Finally Mama breaks down and purchases a little set of blocks, which I assemble and reassemble a thousand times. At night we all place bricks in the oven of the kitchen stove. Prior to going to bed these bricks, one for every family member, are wrapped in paper and placed into the beds before retiring; at first to heat the upper part of the bed and then they are pushed down to the feet keeping them warm. In the mornings everyone gets dressed near the warm kitchen stove and my mother takes my undershirt preheating it by hanging it over the stove railing.

My sisters are allowed to go sledding or join their friends from school sliding on the ice, but at least I have grandma who reads to me or tells me fairy stories, providing entertainment and nourishment for my little mind, while at the same time instilling in me early on a great love for books.

The following spring trouble starts between my mother and my beloved Oma, I don't know why, as well as between my parents. That is the beginning of a long and most stressful time in my life. It inflicts emotional pain but at the same time feeds the longing to leave and explore the outside world.

The atmosphere in the house is growing increasingly tense between Mama and Oma until my grandparents are asked to leave. A particular occurrence can still bring me to tears if I think of it, for I love my grandparents so deeply, yet I do not dare disobey my mother, who has at this point forbidden me to even talk to my grandparents.

It is shortly before they move out and I will see them for the very last time, since both of them die the following year. On a Sunday afternoon my mother has scolded me for some minor annoyance and sensitive as I am, I stand outside crying. My grandparents are just returning from their daily walk and seeing her granddaughter in distress, Oma approaches me and asks gently: "What is the matter child?" Feeling like my heart is being torn apart I move away from the person I love most in the world and hide in the shed, where I sob uncontrollably. I truly hope grandma understands but I still feel terribly guilty. How I would have loved to bury my face into the folds of grandma's long dress and hold on to her for comfort. But I am so afraid of being scolded yet again. The desire to please and not cause any trouble by now is embedded deeply inside me. Unfortunately I have overheard remarks, which make it clear that were it not for me, Papa and Mama would separate and go their own ways.

With my grandparents leaving, a chapter in my young life has ended. It leaves me feeling less grounded than ever before and marks the onset of ever increasing anxiety and worry. Even though I do not know at the time what a Tumbleweed is or even looks like, now it truly becomes part of my heart, soul and mind, taking root firmly and prompting me to pursue the sense of freedom and adventure I will follow later on. I long to be carried away by the wind, far, very far away and the TUMBLEWEED begins to sprout.

Opa

Oma

Feeling guilty

After my grandparents leave, the relationship between my parents continues to deteriorate and weigh heavily on me until I take wing at the age of 22, boarding an airplane bound for New York. But that is a long time away and so I suffer through the vicious arguments that erupt like a volcano at regular intervals and render my life painful.

On a particular morning my father returns totally exhausted from the nightshift at the glass factory when one of these unresolved arguments from the previous day is resumed, as I wake up in the morning lying between my parents. By now I know well that these fights hurt me much deeper than my stepsisters, because it is my father.

Likewise I understand, that I have been conceived and born to keep him from returning to his first wife and children who live in East Germany. I know, because I have heard it often enough. Had it not been for the war, my mother would still live happily with her first husband in a pretty brownstone in Cologne and now she has another child and feels trapped in the relationship. The resulting guilt rests like lead on my tiny shoulders.

That particular morning the ugly words which are being said wash over me like a flood, drowning me in angst and utter despair. I have tried so hard to be as good a little girl as I can possibly be, but whenever the ugly words come to an end I hear: "If it were not for me, Papa would leave or Mama would leave." How then is it possible for my sensitive mind to deduct anything else but that I am the reason for my parents' unhappiness. As the angry words cut deep into my very soul that morning, I cannot be quiet any longer. I start shaking uncontrollably; the emotional pain is so bad. I cry and beg them to stop, telling them while sobbing that I cannot take any more.

I just want to die, run away or plain disappear! After all, isn't it my entire fault? "See what you did," Papa says, "you got the child all upset." Then they quarrel over who has gotten me upset. After a while they are quiet, an angry silence that can almost be felt physically.

I continue to have trouble falling asleep and when I do, I dream of being suspended over a muddy dark pond on a wobbly wooden bridge, which is about to break apart at any moment and I will fall. The reoccurring dream terrifies me, but it keeps coming back over and over again. Eventually I will understand intellectually that indeed I am not at fault.

I am precariously suspended on that wobbly bridge which is the relationship between my parents, but the enormous emotional pain and the scars they form will be with me for the rest of my life.

There are pleasant experiences and I try to recall them in order to offset the pain. One day, when I am almost five, Papa brings home an old bicycle for me, which has been given to him by a friend. He has adjusted the seat for me and we go out to the dirt path in front of our property, him holding me by the back seat and me peddling, while needing constant reassurance that he is holding on. Before I am aware he has let go, and I am riding all by herself. He compliments me to no end, a proud father of a little girl who has learned to ride a bike in record time. It feels wonderful!

Then there are the weekly visits of the baker and the milkman. Since I do not care for milk any longer, his visit is not much anticipated. My mother gives me the old dented milk can and some money. Then I wait patiently by the side of the dirt path and he eventually comes, pours a liter of the fresh white liquid into the can, which I then carry carefully, without spilling, into the shack, where Mama immediately boils it, since it is not pasteurized. Sometimes, if mother is busy, it boils over and makes a terrific mess on the stove, smelling up the entire place with its nauseating odor. I hold my nose or go outside into the fresh air.

The baker on the other hand is quite a different matter. A black horse of medium size drawing a black wagon stops by, and Mama takes me by the hand to see what is available as well as affordable. The delicious smell of fresh bakery goods once the back doors of the wagon opens, makes my mouth water every time. My mother carefully looks for the best rye loaves she can find. If there is enough money left over, she purchases a sweet roll for her youngest daughter. Remembering the smell and taste brings back happy memories!

Since we live so far away from any neighbors and my father works nights each month for an entire week, he decides a good watchdog is needed for protection.

One day he comes home with a German shepherd. It is not a friendly dog. He is chained outside to a doghouse, and every time I try to get close to him he snarls at me, causing me to back up quickly. I slowly resigned myself to the fact that this is not a pet. Even though I would love to have a dog to play with, this dog's stay is short-lived, since he turns out to be a poor example of a watchdog, sleeping all night and never barking when a stranger approaches. That is the end of my dog experience for now.

Oftentimes my mother gives me a note of paper on which she has written items she needs from the store in the next village. She wraps some money into the shopping list, and sends me along the field path all the way to the village to purchase the required items. I just love walking through the fields all by myself, totally unafraid watching the meadow larks take wing singing cheerfully, as well as admiring the multitude of wild flowers in the grain fields along the path. It makes me feel very grown-up when handing over the list to the salesgirl. Then I watch as the required flour, sugar or other items are taken from large bins, weighed on a scale and wrapped into paper bags. Subsequently I carry the purchased goods back home in a shopping net, resting now and then if the content of the net is too heavy.

Every season brings with it something to look forward to which I absorb like a sponge to survive the emotional pain that is my curse. It may be something as simple as being allowed to wear knee socks for the very first time after a winter of scratchy, long woolen stockings attached to uncomfortable garters on my undershirt. Such an occurrence is one of these small joys. So is watching for the first snowdrops and crocuses to appear because that means spring. The hatching of the baby chicks is a most eagerly anticipated event, because I am always allowed to hold the little fuzzy chicks that have hatched and my mother takes out from under the mother hen, so they will not be hurt.

They are then placed into a little old sowing basket and kept warm by the stove. I am allowed to play with them once they are dry and delight in gently touching the fuzzy baby chicks, feeling their little warm bodies nestled in my small hands. Later I love watching the mother hen teach and protect her baby chicks, keeping me busy for hours.

The spring I will be five my father brings home a baby Bantam chick which he gives to me as a pet. I raise it all by myself, carrying it in my apron pocket and it becomes so tame, that it follows me everywhere and is even allowed to take a nap with me. The memory of the little colorful

31

chicken gently pecking at my long eyelashes when it is time to wake up is the beginning of my love for anything with feathers. The little hen follows me everywhere like a dog, and I am happy to have my very own pet. Unfortunately one day the little chicken is missing and is not found until a year later. Apparently it hopped onto the potato crate in the basement and fell behind the space between the crate and the wall, since my mother finds its mummified remains when cleaning out the basement. I grieve a long time for my little chicken friend, the first pet ever that was just mine.

The regular chickens we keep are not as much fun but I certainly enjoy the fine eggs they lay as well as a chicken dinner on a Sunday. It is my father's duty to kill the chicken cutting its head off with an ax on a chopping block reserved for that purpose. While I do enjoy eating the chicken for dinner, I hate when Papa has to kill a chicken and so does he.

Usually the chicken is one of the older ones, which has started to slow down laying eggs. The previous night it is separated from the rest of the flock and when Papa has to perform his least favorite task I usually hide and stick my fingers in my ears so I do not have to hear the chicken's desperate calls. Mama does not seem to mind. Once the chicken has been bled she dunks it into boiling hot water, plucks the feathers and removes the insides saving the heart and gizzards to make chicken soup. Every time I avoid passing the bloodied chopping block for days. Talking to Papa about this I know how much he dislikes cutting off the chickens' heads. Once Mama catches a little wild rabbit and we keep it in a hutch feeding it well to fatten it up. I love the rabbit and can stroke it, so when the day arrives for rabbit stew I cry. Papa kills it by breaking its neck.

Afterwards I hear him telling Mama never to ask him to do that again. He would rather go without meat than having to kill a fuzzy little rabbit. Papa loves animals the way I do because as a child he had no toys at all, and he enjoyed playing with the farm animals.

The summer always brings a lot of rain and sometimes violent thunderstorms which last for hours, being pushed back by the cooler air over the Rhine river. Then we take shelter in the basement, where I feel safe from the thunder and lightening. Mama always takes all the important documents with her, placing them in a big brown leather bag, a leftover habit from the bombing raids and the war. I remember the musty smell of the potato crate and the big dusty coal bin. Once the storms pass and the family ventures back upstairs, I delight in jumping barefoot in the warm puddles, collecting balls of hail and take in the unforgettable fragrance of a summer rain. Frequently there is a rainbow and I make a wish on it. The wish is for peace in the family as well as for my constant anxiety to disappear. I do not know it is called anxiety, all I know is that I am afraid a lot and feel bad, sometimes for no reason at all.

By now the berry bushes my father planted are starting to bear fruit and since there is no candy, fruit becomes one of my favorite snacks. There are strawberries, gooseberries, black and red currants, raspberries and even the cherry trees start to yield a little fruit. Mama allows me to eat as much fruit as I want, and sometimes my cheeks look like those of a chipmunk, full of cherries. I spit out the pits counting how many I have managed to cramp into my mouth. There are pleasant memories of long summer evenings permeated with the sweet smell of ripening grain all around and the haunting song of a distant nightingale. I catch plenty of fireflies and watch the stars before bedtime. All these wonders of nature are absorbed and help to soothe my anxious mind somewhat; my love for the wonders of nature sustains me as much as food.

Autumn brings another special treat. One day, out of no where or so it seams, I can see in the distance a figure dressed in a long black coat and a wide brimmed hat, followed by hundreds of sheep. "The shepherd is coming, the shepherd is coming," I call out excitedly and run to meet him. He is a quiet, middle-aged man of tall stature with kind eyes, moving slowly with his staff and dogs among his sheep. It is obvious to him that his arrival is always eagerly anticipated and he makes it a point to take some time out to talk to me. Every time he allows me to pet as many sheep as I wish and every fall he spends one night in the large field adjacent to my family's property. It seems to me that there is no end to the field of gentle sheep. Their bleating has a calming effect on me and I sleep well on those nights. Those are the nights my world seems to be in order.

As it grows colder and the first frost settles on the asters and dahlias, Papa grows the most beautiful and largest dahlias on earth, sometimes my world turns into a breathtaking picture from one of my favorite fairy tales by Hans Christian Andersen, the "Snow Queen." It usually disappears by midmorning but I imagine myself in the fairy tale, which my dear Oma read to me so many times. Once the frost comes hard I amuse myself by sliding on the ice which has formed on the numerous puddles of the dirt path or braking it. I stomp hard and it shatters like glass under my feet. As it gets closer to Christmas, I often sit on my swing in the late afternoon watching the sun set, turning the sky a brilliant red. I have been told it is then that the Christchild and the angels are baking Christmas cookies. In my daydreaming I see the big ovens and busy angels hard at work baking Christmas cookies for all the children in the world.

While I still miss my grandparents desperately, I am not allowed to ask or talk about them and so I miss them silently in my heart.

Thank God there is Tante Grete, my favorite aunt and a constant positive presence in my life. Being a widow, she comes to visit frequently on weekends and is always a participant for the holidays. Christmas in particular is simply unimaginable without Tante Grete's presence, since she helps with the preparations for the holiday feast, which usually consists of a stuffed goose and many of the canned summer treasures, carefully stored away in the basement on a great many shelves. Yes, Tante Grete is a very special person in my life and now, as a grown woman, I realize why I feel about her the way I do. There are many character traits we share. But that again does not become clear to me until I grow up and pay her a visit prior to leaving Germany for good. By then Tante Grete had moved back to Cologne after a falling out with Mama.

Even though, to my great dismay, I find her living in what was left over from a pre-war building, basically a fixed-up ruin and rather shabby from the outside, her apartment itself is cozy as always. For the special occasion of her niece's visit she offers some delicacies and we sit together chatting about the "good old times." Then she sends me on my way with her best wishes, an armload full of new towels and bed sheets as well as a good cook book, which I use even now when cooking German dishes 32 years later. I treasure it like I treasure the memory of my aunt who was so instrumental in my early years. Someone I could always turn to for advice and help after my grandparents were removed from my life so heartlessly. Tante Grete proved to be one of the most resilient people I have ever known, and I am pleased that after all the heartaches and difficulties this tiny woman had endured, she eventually just slipped away quietly in her sleep at the ripe old age of 89. Mind you, she was a smoker of strong German unfiltered cigarettes all of her life, despised exercise and loved to eat any type of fatty meat without given the slightest consideration ever to cholesterol levels. With a little brandy for digestive purposes now and then she remained self-sufficient to the very end, indulging in her passion for reading good books, listening to good music and doing the finest needle-work. Nor did she ever give the impression of being lonely. While she was happy to receive visitors, she was never unhappy to see them leave; a woman who truly enjoyed her own company. The year prior to her death, on the occasion of a visit to my parents and nursing my mother back from surgery, I visit Tante Grete and am asked if there is anything in particular I would like to have to remember her by. We are able to talk about such matters freely and, while looking around her apartment, an old pewter bird which I remember playing with as a child catches my eye. "Yes," I say, "the old vulture, I would like that." Tante Grete corrects me as she always does: "That is a Marabu my dear, I will put it aside and tell your sister about it." Then we share one of Tante Grete's strong cups of coffee which always give me heart palpitations and enjoy some delicious German crème cake I picked up at the bakery prior to my visit. Six months later my much loved aunt just peacefully slips away one night in her own bed; a mystery to modern medicine.

While on my next visit the following year, I ask my sister for the keepsake which Tante Grete promised me. The response is cold and final: "I have that and I am not willing to part with it. I have it standing on my coffee table but I will look to see if there is some old silver left." "Never mind," I reply, but the painful feeling, which rises up in me like bile does not leave me for a long time. Once again I feel like the outsider, nothing has really changed during all that time. I am glad to realize that the decision to leave and give up my German citizenship was the best thing I ever did! It probably saved my life and my sanity.

Tante Grete

Big Changes

After my grandparents depart, we now receive visitors from East Germany once in a while. They are amongst others my paternal grandfather, a stern man of whom I remember little, other than having to be on my best behavior. He has a large handlebar moustache, its gray coarse hair twirled upwards. We never exchange many words. I remember him coming for a visit after staying with my father's youngest brother who, after spending a year in Great Britain as a prisoner of war, ended up marrying my mother's sister 20 years his senior (a union happier than most I have seen during my life).

There is no outward sign of affection between my generally affectionate father and my grandfather. The abuse he had to endure as a child and the memory of how his gentle mother had suffered, cause him to dislike his own father intensely. Especially when drunk, my paternal grandfather had reacted to the slightest sign of disobedience, even if only perceived as such, with the most violent temper until at the age of 18, when Papa had grown into a strong young man. Then he had held his father's arms telling him never to lay a hand on him again. And he had not. Another thing Papa could not forgive his father for was the fact that he had been a very bright and studious child who had been sent to high school upon the teacher's urging, intending to later pursue a career in the visual arts. It had been his dream to attend the Art Institute in Berlin and to become a painter. However his father had taken him out of school at the age of 14 and arranged for him to become an apprentice to a housepainter and wallpaper hanger. Although he received no formal training, in later years Papa painted beautiful oil paintings of flowers and landscapes which grace my home today. Nonetheless, it had been one of the greatest, most cruel disappointments in his life. I remember him telling me that, even when standing at his father's grave, he could not shed a tear. There were too many hard feelings bottled up inside him. Even prior to his own death, at the ripe old age of 82, he would tell me the sad stories of his own youth. Apparently my paternal grandmother who died prior to my birth, had been a pretty girl, working in Berlin for a Jewish family as a maid, where she had learned cooking, sowing and many things which she appreciated. The family had been very good to her and even provided her with plenty of gifts when she got married to my grandfather. He had been stationed in Berlin while undergoing his mandatory training in the army. Grandmother, having been raised in the city, never anticipated how hard her life would be married to a mason and living in the countryside without running water and all the conveniences she was used to. In addition she had given birth to one child after another in quick succession and become the object of her husband's wrath when he was drunk. All I have of her is one photograph taken in 1914, showing a handsome young women with her three oldest sons, my father being the third of five, plus there were two sisters, one of whom died of pneumonia at the age of four. I know that she had a tender heart and that her favorite flower was the bleeding heart. Today there is a bleeding heart growing by my front door.

Other than my grandfather from the East, there are visits from my uncles, my father's brothers, their wives and sometimes my cousins. The East German Government is very clever. In order to prevent people from not returning, families are not allowed to travel together. Thus we are either visited by the uncles and aunts or by my cousins.

While I like my uncles and aunts, there is a problem with space and I hate having to sleep between my relatives on the proverbial "Besuchersritze" (visitor's slot). They snore, smell strangely and I really am not comfortable with the arrangement at all, come to think of, I never did find out where my parents slept when we had visitors.

The following spring big changes begin to take place. Since the amount of refugees from the East is overwhelming and the cities still lie in ruins, the resulting shortage of housing makes it necessary for the new German Government under Konrad Adenauer to provide low interest loans for the building of new home developments. One of those developments is planned and constructed right across from my family's little homestead, and with all the construction that destroys the serenity and quiet I had taken from nature, there is one big fringe benefit. Along with the development come children my own age, the construction of a new elementary school as well as a Catholic Church.

The area changes drastically. Streets are built and with that come electricity and water. Construction equipment is everywhere, piling up huge mountains of earth which are fun to climb on. Then, one day, I meet the new neighbors across the street, who just happen to have a little son my age. We become friends immediately and once he moves in we become inseparable. Dieter is the first friend I ever have.

Little do I realize the impact that friendship would have in the future, since his uncle ended up marrying my oldest stepsister and turned out to be a physically and mentally abusive alcoholic. Combined with the traumatic war experiences of my sister, this causes her to suffer a mental breakdown from which she never quite recovers. The last time I saw my old childhood friend was on the occasion of another visits to my parents in 1992. We got together to fill each other in on the years there had been no contact whatsoever. By then he was married for the second time to an Iranian woman and had moved back into his parents' home across the street. After his father's death his mother hanged herself in the basement of their house from a sewer pipe. I remember asking if it did not bother him to live in the house where his mother had taken her own life, but he was in the process of remodeling and apparently able to deal with this tragedy. I do not think I could live there without haunting memories. But then people deal differently with life's blows and considering my background, my ability to cope with stress is sadly inadequate.

Looking back I remember his father and mother as they were when I was just a child; a good-natured young man and a dark-haired young woman whose tragic end no one could have imagined. We used to play in the basement of their house with Dieter's little steam factory as well as hide and seek on rainy days, but now it takes on a dark dimension due to a woman's desperate last act.

With the school, the church and the many houses, the new little village also attracts a grocery store, a bakery and a butcher shop. The school opens just in time, since law requires for children to enter first grade at the age of six.

I look forward to learning how to read, since no one in my family has taken the time my grandmother did reading stories to me, an experience I sorely miss. Once in school I can learn how to read and be able to do so any time I wish, an idea, which excites me to no end. Running errands for my mother is easier as well. No longer do I have to walk for miles with my little shopping list. However there is one

41

thing I did not anticipate. With the influx of people and new homes, I suddenly feel that people look down on my family: the people living in the shack. Shortly thereafter I also find out the hard way what it means to be of illegitimate birth and the stigma attached to this fact back then.

One afternoon Mama sends me to the local grocery store with a list of items she needs.

When I innocently enter the store three women and the shopkeeper are present. With my entry the conversation stops abruptly and one of the women turns around and asks me: "What is your name?" Taught to be polite by my parents I answer dutifully. The next question comes from the second woman: "What is your mother's name?" Likewise I answer beginning to feel slightly uncomfortable when I notice the smirk on their faces.

Then of course the last question comes: "What is your father's name?" I tell them, now fully aware at this point that I am the target of vicious ridicule, since they are three different last names. I turn around and leave the store in tears. When I arrive back home without the items I was supposed to purchase, I refuse to tell my mother why. Later that night I tell my father what happened and ask never to be sent back to that store again. He talks to my mother because I never again set foot in the place where I was forced to endure such humiliation. It does not stop there though. The new priest makes it a point to visit my mother and requests my father move out, since she is living in sin with a married man. My mother asks the priest to leave and other than on the occasion of my First Communion and the funeral of some of her friends, she never sets foot in a church again. The war experience had robbed her of her faith and while she makes her girls attend church every

Sunday, she has a hard time believing in a God who allowed the cruelty she witnessed and survived.

More arguments follow and my father tries his best to get a divorce but the East German Government will not grant it. Thus his hands are tied. My sisters are also ridiculed, but at least they carry my mother's name while I have three different names to cope with. The trouble with sleepless nights continues and by now I have also started to walk in my sleep.

That Christmas though, I still remember as the best I ever experienced. I have an Adventskalender made of paper with little doors to open and adorned with silver sparkles showing the Christchild with his angel helpers descending from heaven. Every day I open a little door and marvel at the pretty picture inside. No peeking allowed, or the Christchild will not come, I am told. Finally it is December 24 and Christmas Eve, the time when children in Germany receive their Christmas presents.

According to tradition, children are not allowed in the living room until Christmas Eve. All day long I have been nervous in anticipation and restless, getting on Mama's nerves and being sent out to play on numerous occasions. But it is rainy and cold, simply miserable outside, with nothing at all to do but wonder about Christmas.

Finally it is time for dinner. After getting dressed in our Sunday clothes a little glass bell rings in the living room and the door opens wide. I stand in the doorway mesmerized by the most beautiful Christmas tree I have ever seen. Naturally it is lit with real candles, decked out with homemade decorations such as walnuts dipped in golden color, glass icicles which Papa has fashioned by himself while at the glass factory and pieces of candy wrapped in colorful foil. What really takes my breath away is the fact that the tree seems to be exploding with sparklers, since they are suspended at the tips of its outer branches and the colorful spectacle, even though it only lasts a few minutes, is pure magic to a little girl. Once I have said my Christmas prayer I am allowed to look under the tree and there I find a wicker doll carriage with a miniature feather bed and pillow of bright red and white gingham, each of them with a pretty ruffle.

Inside the doll carriage there is my old doll Marlene, who has been outfitted with a new head and hand-made clothes in pink. She wears a dress, a cape, a bonnet and even tiny socks and shoes. It definitely is the best Christmas present I have ever received. For a little while all my troubles blend into the background and I feel real bliss.

In later years I find out that my father had walked for miles, then taken a train into Cologne, which was still mostly a pile of rubble with just a few open department stores, and spent what was then a fortune for the pretty and sturdy doll carriage. Proudly he had carried it home for his little girl. Tante Grete had knitted the clothes for the doll, my mother had made the bedding and picked out a new head for Marlene, which from then on is renamed Susanne. It is the most beautiful and peaceful Christmas I ever recall when I still believed in the coming of the Christchild.

School Starts

In the spring of 1953 I am eagerly looking forward to my first day of school. When it finally comes I am very nervous and lean heavily on my friend across the street. I wake up early and get dressed in my Sunday dress, also knitted by Tante Grete. My long blond hair in loose pigtails with bows, I proudly put on my Tornister, the leather book bag German schoolchildren carry on their backs. In it there is a slate with a sponge attached and it contains a small case of "Griffel," items one uses to write with on a slate. I examine everything carefully and notice that one side of the slate is lined, while the other side is marked with squares, meaning one side is for writing and the other side for numbers. Just prior to leaving for my first day of school Mama presents me with the traditional German gift for this special occasion, a "Zuckertuete." This is a cone-shaped cardboard container, covered on the outside with colorful shiny paper and on the inside filled with fruit, candy and cookies. I receive a red one to match the color of my dress and proudly make my way on my mother's hand to the brand new school, which is within easy walking distance.

Altogether there are 38 children in my class and the teacher is a kind young woman by the name of Mrs. Mueller. After the traditional school picture of the class has been taken, we follow the teacher into our classroom where Dieter and I take seats together, since the benches are designed for two pupils. The teacher explains the rules, we receive our first lesson and are given a homework assignment.

I take to school and learning like a fish to water. When I return home that first day not only do I complete my assignment but I do twice as much as is required. Looking back I have to smile, admitting to myself that I have always been a typical overachiever.

School is great fun and I enjoyed recess, when all children are allowed to go outside, eat their sandwich and then play. Even though I have grown up socially isolated, now I blend in with ease and made friends quickly. Nevertheless, no one will ever take the place of Dieter. By the end of the first week I visit the library. Even though I am unable to spell my last name, I proudly check out the book of my choice and Mrs. Mueller, who that day doubles as the librarian after school, is astounded but hands me the book with a smile.

Shortly after that day the teacher visits my mother because she has taken a personal interest in me, this inquisitive child. However, she has also noticed that something is amiss. The little girl is obviously suffering from stress and overly eager to please at any price. The teacher shows concern for my wellbeing and discusses different issues with my mother.

The book I take out of the school library is about a little girl my age whose doll is stolen by Gypsies. I remember that my sisters get very impatient with me, since I am only able to read the little words and have to ask for help constantly with the larger ones. But eventually I make my way through the book, and from then on I am a constant visitor at the school library.

The teacher is extremely kind to me and even invites me and my best friend to her apartment for afternoon hot chocolate and cookies. On that occasion we find out that the young teacher is married to a high school art teacher. Together we admire his paintings.

Their apartment, located on the second floor of the Principal's house adjacent to the elementary school, is very cozy. The Principal's hobby is bee-keeping and whenever I see a honeybee in our garden, my father tells me it is one from Mr. Koppelberg's hive. When I ask him how he knows he laughs and teases me saying: "don't you notice the K on its back?" For the longest time I believe him and to this day, the first thing I think of when I see a honeybee, is Mr. Koppelberg and his beehives. It is one of those memories that come to mind even before conscious thought takes over.

The first year of school goes well. I have even been chosen for the lead role of the school play, Snow-White, to play the princess, with Dieter playing the role of the prince.

47

Inge Perreault

It is performed on the occasion of a school trip to the Fairy Tale Forest in Altenberg, being attended by most parents and proves to be a great success. Even Papa can attend because he has a day off and I truly feel like a little princess for once.

In years to come I will return to the Fairy Tale Forest many times, visiting this special place with my own children. It is located about 20 miles from where I live in a small mountain range in the town of Altenberg, which also houses an ancient Dom (cathedral) and a monastery. The Fairy Tale Forest is pure magic. A dirt path winds itself along the Valley with a gurgling brook, slightly upward and surrounded by a dense pine forest. At certain intervals there are little buildings, already then quite old when I first see them at the age of 6, depicting scenes from my beloved fairy tales by the Bothers Grimm.

You can peek inside the small houses; all of them build to resemble the time the fairy tales originated and quite ornate, scaled to the size of children. We marvel at the porcelain life-like figures of the many characters in a surrounding of antique furniture and décor. There is a picture of me somewhere, peeking out of the window of the Gingerbread House from the fairy tale "Hansel and Gretel" (you can go inside where it is scary, dark and the witch is checking up on the poor children held prisoner here) as well as one of my youngest son taken 30 years later, looking out of the very same little window. Everyone loves the Fairy Tale Forest, neither my children nor I will ever forget it and I can only hope that it does not fall into disrepair or is replaced by a modern Disneyland. The little houses are so charming, unless you see it for yourself it is difficult to convey the experience. There is the tower in which Rapunzel is held captive, and when calling out "Rapunzel,

Rapunzel, let down your hair" a long blond braid of hair descends and the face of a pretty girl peeks out of the top of the tower. There is Puss in Boots, the characters from the most loved fairy tales as well as some displays which are special to the larger Cologne region and every child has been told about.

Then we have lunch at the restaurant where, at the end, we get to listen to a beautiful piece of classical music and watch a colorful display of water fountains in tune with the symphony. Yes, those are the memories I truly cherish.

However, people being what they are, one day I arrive at school and prior to the teacher's arrival a chant has been started in the classroom teasing me because I live in a wooden shack, while everyone else lives in new houses and I start to cry. The teacher walks in at the right time overhearing what is being chanted and gets very angry. She reprimands the class severely, tells them she has been to visit my house that she does not consider a shack but refers to as a little castle, spotlessly clean and surrounded by flowers, fruit trees and bountiful vegetable gardens. She threatens to punish any child severely if she ever hears such talk again.

Nevertheless, the damage is done and once again the very familiar feeling of not belonging is reinforced. I continue to be the best student in class but start to withdraw from certain children, the instigators of yet another humiliation. The gossip of their parents has been picked up concerning my illegitimacy and they delight in teasing me about the three different names in my family. Every time a paper needs my parents' signature it carries different names and the shame I feel totally negates the fact that the paper is marked with a large "A."

Nevertheless I enjoy school and Mrs. Mueller, my much-admired teacher, continues to be my second as well as third grade teacher. During this time I sleep better than ever before and oftentimes the constant anxiety almost vanishes.

The four week Advent season is always particularly wonderful, since there is an Advent's wreath hanging in each classroom. Every Monday morning the light is turned off, the candles are lit and we sing old German Christmas songs. Since it is dark this early in the morning during the winter, (there is no day-light savings time) the flickering of the candles and the sound of our enthusiastic voices will never be forgotten.

Then the unthinkable happens! Mrs. Mueller gets pregnant and decides to stay home with her baby. Fourth grade is a rude awakening, with an old and very strict male teacher, whose first step to make me dislike him is the separation of boys and girls on different sides of the classroom. Both Dieter and I shed tears on that occasion, for we have sat next to each other for three years and are still inseparable after school.

The only positive thing I remember about that particular spring is the fact that my father is allowed to go back to his old job with the railroad. During Easter vacation he takes his bicycle all the way into Cologne to pick up his uniform. Wanting to take his little daughter with him he installs a small seat in the front of his bicycle and together we set out early in the morning. I remember distinctly his strong hands grabbing the handlebars, hands that perform hard work but which can also be very gentle. Silently I compare them to my mother's hands, once the beautiful hands of a city girl but now marked by house and garden work. If she had only been able to reconcile herself to the fact that she was no longer a pretty pampered city girl and been able to accept my father's country ways, things might have been peaceful, but both of my parents have a stubborn streak and my mother in particular a very unforgiving nature. I do not think she realized the damage she unintentionally inflicted on me because I know she truly loves me.

By lunchtime my father and I reach Cologne and eat our sandwiches on a bench overlooking the Rhine, the Cathedral and the big city which is undergoing the process of reconstruction. There are still many structures in ruins, but the bridges crossing the Rhine connecting both parts of the city have been repaired. Thus we are able to cross. My father finds the regional main office and is issued the proper railroad uniform. When we reach home it is late afternoon but on the way all that day we talk a lot and have a good time.

Since my father has been given a position at the railroad switching station where he is responsible for directing the trains in the proper direction, the uniform is not mandatory.

Other than in one picture, taken for posterity, he never wore it. When asked why, he says that he was forced to wear a uniform during the war long enough and never intends to wear another.

Thinking back of Mrs. Mueller and what later happened in my beloved teacher's life makes clear that she too is a casualty of the Second World War. Even though she moved away after her second daughter was born, she later suffered several nervous breakdowns resulting in a stay at an institution and falls into deep depressions, no doubt the belated reaction to the horrendous war experiences she had endured. It is sad to think of the emotional pain this kind young woman suffered through no fault of her own. But then there are many thousands of such belated civilian war casualties. I think of the mother of my girlfriend Liese, who

51

was raped by a Polish soldier and thus conceived her daughter under very violent circumstances. I spend many afternoons playing at her apartment in the company of her elderly grandfather, who watches his grandchild while her mother works at a local lamp factory. Oftentimes Liese makes up stories about her imaginary father owning an ice cream shop, a candy store or being a famous, if somewhat illusive, person. Her mother, a kind and gentle woman, is another of the many belated victims of the war. Her story in particular has a very sad ending. All her life she sacrificed for her daughter, raised a fine young woman and then one day, years after her daughter had gotten married they had quarreled. Apparently that had been the breaking point for the mother, who had attempted to kill the child she had conceived in violence but loved nevertheless. She entered her daughter's apartment at night and tried to kill her with a hammer. Once she had come to her senses, she herself committed suicide by jumping off one of the Cologne bridges. Her body was later washed ashore 20 kilometers downstream. What a terrible tragedy for both, mother and daughter.

How many silent casualties of innocent victims of circumstances beyond their control were there, I wonder? My own generation seems to be the last to be directly affected by the Second World War and Hitler's terrible legacy. There are probably hundreds of thousands like me if not millions. Looking back at my difficult childhood which left me deeply scarred, there are so many who crossed my path. Stories similar to my experiences and the pain they caused. But no one seemed to care or even try to understand. The German people were guilty of committing terrible war crimes and what happened to millions of innocent people was not even a point of discussion. After all, did they not deserve their fate considering the havoc Hitler had caused? Thus collective guilt was drummed into my mind ever since I can remember, and even today, after having lived in the United States for 32 years and becoming a citizen, I still encounter prejudice and animosity at times.

But in my journey back, trying to make sense of what caused me to become what I am, I resolve to get back to my own life and the events, which shaped me in years to come.

When school resumes that fall it brings with it kite-flying on the harvested wheat fields and digging potatoes with my family for the winter months. The wonderful smell of burning the potato vines and later digging a few potatoes, which have been placed underneath the ashes, tasting delicious once they are cooked.

School itself takes on a new dimension. By now the "baby boom" has become apparent and the school just cannot handle all the children. Consequently two shifts are introduced while an addition is constructed. One week I attend school during the morning hours and the following week during the afternoon. With yet another strict male teacher and the enormous load of homework he likes to give, life becomes exceedingly stressful again.

Likewise life at home, the situation between my parents has taken a turn for the worse, to a point where between the stress at school as well as in my home life endless sleepless nights become the rule again and I begin to faint on a regular basis. At first this starts at church, where all the little children have to sit in front and the pungent smell of incense makes me feel sick. When I try to sit down feeling woozy an elderly woman pokes me in the back. Dutifully I kneel down again on the hard wooden pew.

All I remember after that is a loud noise in my head, falling onto the edge of the wooden pew and hitting the hard marble floor. When I wake up I am being held outside by the wife of the school principal. Mrs. Koppelberg is always a real lady. I remember looking up into her concerned face under the wide brimmed hat she always wears to church. After I recover Mrs. Koppelberg even takes me home and explains to my mother that I fainted.

Following this incidence I develop a phobia of going to church. I hit my head badly and from then on I always sit at the end of the pew looking for a quick exit if I feel unwell. The same begins to happen in school, where I begin to feel in the middle of a lesson like a train is roaring through my head, especially if there is a lot of activity and noise. After I have fainted a couple of times, I ask the teacher to be allowed to go home whenever I experience this feeling. It is the oddest feeling of helplessness and utter panic which makes my head dizzy, my heart race and causes me as well as my parents great distress. A physician is consulted but he cannot find any physical reason for my symptoms. It will take many decades before I am properly diagnosed and medical science acknowledges the condition exists, namely I suffer from Panic Anxiety Disorder, totally unknown back then.

In addition, by now I have also finally found a very effective defense mechanism to make my parents stop fighting. Since during the war and shortly thereafter they had gone hungry, food is extremely important to them. And so it becomes my weapon. I simply refused to eat when there is fighting in the home. It works so well that in time this defense mechanism becomes part of me to the point where I actually am unable to eat or will vomit whenever the stress becomes unbearable, something that in future years will lead to my hospitalization several times.

It is all a very insidious development over the course of years and it will take many years to undo at least part of the damage I suffered so early on in life.

I get prepared for my first Communion when I am almost eight years old. The Rhineland is traditionally an almost exclusively Catholic area. However, since the war the area had gained quite a substantial influx of Lutheran Protestants due to the displaced population from what has become East Germany under Russion control, who have chosen to make a new life for themselves in the West. Since separation of Church and State does not exist; we have religious instructions twice a week in school. While the local Priest instructs Catholic students, a Protestant Minister takes the other children of Protestant faith into another classroom. All this is perfectly normal and poses no problem for the children who form friendships freely amongst each other, and it is only the obsession of the Catholic Priest who succeeds heaping a hefty amount of guilt on us during religious instructions for fraternizing with the "enemy." Since my father is Protestant I disagree in my heart, without letting it be known, for the Priest is an alcoholic with a vicious temper. During Sunday masses fire and brimstone tumble from the pulpit onto the guilt-laden backs of his parishioners and form the core of his sermons. It is not beyond him to slap the cheek of one of the altar boys during mass or stumble in a drunken stupor. There are times I fear he will have a stroke or a heart attack because his face becomes flaming red when he goes into one of his tirades, spewing out his message with spittle flying in obvious disgust of his sinful congregation. However, we are actually not afraid of him. Behind his back we laugh and snicker. We have all seen him at the annual carnival falling down and making a total fool of himself. The following day

55

he can be seen walking through what has now become a village, deeply absorbed in prayer while ever so often checking his bible.

I am very excited about my first Communion. It is a two day affair and entails a big family celebration. My mother buys me the communion dress, white gloves, a crown of white roses for my hair and black patent leather shoes. I have never known such luxury.

We are supposed to have another new Sunday outfit for the second feast day but Papa says it's too expensive and not necessary. I should wear my old Sunday dress. Tante Gete comes to my rescue, takes me into town and buys me another new dress. It is a pretty light blue with a white stripe in the material and I love it. Many years later, when Tante Grete is in her 80s, we will reminisce and she will say:"remember when I bought you your dress for the second day of Communion? I did not want you to feel left out and didn't we have fun together in the store choosing just the right dress?"

"Yes," I say gratefully, "I always have been able to count on you to come through," I tell her how much it meant to me, how much her presence added to my life. Germans are not outwardly affectionate and "I love you" is pretty much reserved for young lovers, so I don't say it but she knows I do!

There will be presents for the special occasion and my most fervent wish is for new handlebars for my old bicycle. My handlebars are totally out of style. Straight modern looking ones are "in" and there is nothing I wish for more than new handlebars. I have to sit back and smile at what a child would say today, if given a new set of handlebars for an old bike, instead of a brand new bicycle. Given today's behavior of children it is difficult for me to imagine the reaction. But then my wants were simple and have always stayed that way, although through hard work God has blessed me in many areas I could not have imagined in my wildest dreams.

Two days prior to my first Communion I have a minor accident. There is a little stream that flows through the village running in a channel lined with concrete. My friends and I have thought up a little game we that call "brook-running," meaning we get down into the channel and run along the cement edges of the brook which slope, skipping back and forth from side to side. Once in a while someone slips and falls into the little stream which is only about a foot deep. It would be my luck to do just that and come running home soaking wet. I can still hear my mother's lamenting about how I will get sick, come down with pneumonia or some dread disease, that no doubt I will spoil the entire upcoming festivities. Naturally I am terrified. My mother is right, how could I have been so stupid and fall into the cold water on a dreary spring day? By now I have internalized the fact that my mother holds me personally responsible for getting sick.

It is always my fault. Consequently my nerves are frazzled with fear about falling ill. But I don't, and my first Communion turns out to be a festive and enjoyable day, the only time I ever remember being in a German Church with my mother. Everybody is dressed in their best Sunday clothes and the traditional garland of white paper roses adorns the entrance door to the shack.

However on that day it does not matter, in particular since the foundation for a new house has been completed and the cement blocks have already been delivered.

The previous winter my parents decided to take the big step and build a new house.

All of us were involved in the design aspect and once the architect has drawn up the final plans the required building permits are obtained and the excavation starts. My mother took her widow's pension in one lump sum and thus enabled my parents to purchase the necessary materials. My father, the son of a mason, will build the house almost entirely by himself with my mother by his side handing him the proper tools, keeping the cost within what the family can afford. So I can see an end to my days of living in a wooden shack and being teased about it.

Not being able to eat prior to receiving my first Communion almost makes me faint but I make it through the service and after a hearty breakfast at home I can open my presents. At last, there they are, the much longed for handlebars for my bike. They are shiny chrome with yellow accents and I am quite sure they are the most beautiful handlebars I have ever seen. My oldest sister and her new husband present me with this gift. Dieter's uncle has recently married my oldest sister in a small civil ceremony.

Frankly, I cannot even remember having a celebration for their wedding. The only thing I do remember is seeing them both tipsy after drinking too much wine.

My Communion lunch, the biggest meal of the day, consists of a big feast and for once the family, that is my parents, my sisters, my new brother-in-law, Tante Grete and a few of my parents' friends enjoy a peaceful day. That is so very rare in my house, it truly stands out in my mind. And I did not even get sick. The other gifts I receive are clothes, books and some money. I love the books and begin reading that day while holding onto my new handlebars. The next day I will drive my father crazy begging him to install them on my old bike, but it will have to wait because he has to go to work.

Mostly the second Communion Day is for the children. I attend Church by myself in my new dress from Tante Grete, still wearing my crown of white roses, receive Communion again and sit through an entire lengthy mass. We suspect the Priest is making it especially long just to annoy us, for he basically does not show much love or tolerance for children. Afterwards we are free to go and in the afternoon I am allowed to give a party for my friends with cake, hot chocolate and sweets. Then we are sent outside to play and have fun. I remember my first Communion fondly and two days later I am proudly riding my old bicycle with my NEW HANDLEBARS.

Now I am expected to take Communion at least once a month and go to confession the day before. What does a child like me have to confess? I have to think really hard and usually come up with the same list of items, such as having had unkind thoughts, having not honored my elders, having told a little lie. It is difficult because I try so very much to be good and please, because the last thing I want to do is cause any more trouble by my sheer existence than I already seem to do.

One Saturday afternoon when I go to confession the full wrath of God seems to come down on the Priest; at least that is what I think. My friends and I are waiting in the pews pondering our sins while he is in the confessional. By now we are used to the fact that sometimes he falls asleep and after confessing we have to cough or make a noise to wake him up. Then he tells us our penance which always seems to consist of two "Our Father's" and three "Hail Mary's." Oftentimes I wonder if somebody does something really bad, will he still get the same penance and does the Priest have a soft spot in his heart for the Virgin Mary? Those are the thoughts that go around in my head while waiting for my turn to confess.

On this particular afternoon workmen are present in the Church and in the process of hoisting a huge tapestry about 40 feet in length on the back-wall of the Church behind the altar. The Priest is obviously preoccupied and keeps peeking out of the confessional frequently, plus he is not happy with the entire process since it is not being hoisted up straight but one side is lower than the other. All of a sudden he cannot stand it any longer.

In the middle of my girlfriend Liese's confession he comes bursting out of the confessional, his face red and marked by anger he goes to the workmen and starts to yell at them loudly. We all sit quietly waiting what will happen next and then the unthinkable does happen. God punishes the Priest for his unkindness right in front of our eyes as we watch the process unfold. Suddenly one rope used to hoist the heavy tapestry gives way and within seconds the Priest is covered completely under the heavy cloth. Since he is of small stature it is comical to see him struggle underneath trying to free himself. We all look at each other and begin to giggle (behind our hands so he will not hear us) because it is the funniest sight any of us have ever seen. Even the workmen who jumped out of the way just in time laugh and we know that they are having the exact same thought: serves him right!

Once the Priest struggles out from under his confinement he yells at the workmen some more, then storms back into the confessional and we all receive double penance that day. Once outside, all of us agree it was worth it though. There is a God and he does punish unkindness, even in a Priest.

In fourth grade I start taking English lessons on a voluntary basis and I thoroughly enjoy it. It gives me a strange feeling of freedom to be able to converse in a language nobody else in my family understands. I also notice that I learn another language easily without much effort, and that my pronunciation lacks the usual heavy German accent.

While the fact of my illegitimacy is still a very unpleasant aspect of my life, for now I try to ignore innuendoes and unkind remarks.

The time that is not taken up with schoolwork is spent roller-skating. Since the roads are paved now my mother has purchased a pair of roller skates, the kind which are clamped to the soles of your shoes and ruin them. For at least a year I basically live on roller skates in my spare time. Setting out from my house I pick up my friend across the street, then we proceed to pick up other classmates on the following cross streets until we have enough kids together to play a variety of games. I teach myself to skate backwards and can actually do so for very long distances. Once I have mastered the skill I teach the others and we invent new games. During this period I skate so much that to my parents' dismay I ruin several pairs of shoes and eventually the metal wheels of the rollers have holes in them. That is the end of my roller skating adventures!

I do not receive any type of allowance, however I deliver fresh eggs once a week to a couple in the next village on my bike. The people own a Newspaper/Candy Store and are always very nice to me, allowing me to go into the store and pick out a piece of candy as well as giving me an extra 10 Pfennig each time which I save diligently. After two years I have enough money saved to order myself a dress from a Catalogue. It feels wonderful to be able to pick out the dress I want, whether it is practical or not.

That year I also go on my first vacation ever. My sister takes me along on her vacation for two weeks to the Black Forest. We take the train and change in Freiburg boarding another one which takes us to our final destination, Hinterzarten. Located in the heart of the Black Forest Region within hiking distance of the highest mountain, the Feldberg and a nice lake, the Tittisee, we lodge in an ancient farmhouse with hand-hewn timbers and a roof which almost reaches all the way to the ground. The house actually dates back to the seventeenth century. These old farmhouses are quite charming and practical since due to the harsh winters in this area, the cattle as well as the hayloft all form part of the farmhouse. The farmer rents out rooms during the summer months for additional income. The cost includes breakfast which we are supposed to take in the dining room where there is a huge old Kachelofen in one corner, a tile covered built-in stove reaching from floor to ceiling, quite ornate and surrounded by a bench.

But I cannot stand the smell of the cows and fresh milk, which permeates this room since the cows are housed just across the hall.

Consequently, after getting sick to my stomach several times, we take our breakfast in our room at a cozy little table by the corner window that overlooks the valley. It is very peaceful and I am grateful to my sister for having taken me along, though I did not know that she would also meet up with her boyfriend, later to become her husband. On hikes I always have to go ahead so they can walk behind me and hold hands, stopping ever so often to exchange a kiss. I am not stupid and catch on rather fast. It also occurs to me that my future brother-in-law has a serious character defect, namely he is selfish in that he eats most of the food we order, whether I am still hungry or not. Unfortunately at this time my sister is blind to this fault, a fact that many years later will come between them and lead to a rather stormy marriage. All in all we have a good time though, I make friends with the farmer's children and the farmer even takes me along on the hay wagon.

By the time we leave I have adopted the Black Forest dialect and accent, further proof of my talent for languages. During the last week of our vacation I unfortunately catch a cold even though I always carried a sweater with me. So on my return I am questioned by my mother as to why I caught a cold. I am never allowed to question her when she takes sick. It makes me wonder why she always blames me, yet never accepts any responsibility for her own illnesses. In fact she quite often conveniently blames them on my father or me.

All in all I prove to be a sickly child. When chicken pox catches up with me they hit me hard. It is one of those nights when Papa works the night shift and I am allowed to sleep in his bed. During the night I dream of the Carmelite Nuns I was so afraid of years ago, swooping down on me like giant birds in their strange garb. When I awaken from my nightmare I am sweating with fever, my head aches terribly and I feel the blisters on my face. As is usual by now, once again I am stricken with a disease in early

November, which prevents me from taking part in the traditional St. Martin's parade. On the eve of St. Martin's Day all schoolchildren meet at the village center, where during the day the men of the fire department have erected a bonfire. There the procession will begin with "St. Martin" on horseback leading the children who carry lanterns glowing in the dark November evening through the village streets. The procession culminates back at the bonfire where, prior to lighting it, St. Martin delivers a speech on charity. Then the school children walk to their school building, where they receive a "Weckmann," a type of gingerbread man made of sweet dough with raisins for eyes and a clay pipe in one arm.

After that the most beautiful lantern is judged. If I remember correctly I am able to take part in the parade only a couple of times since I am mostly ill. Once, when in first grade, my father carried me wrapped in blankets to the sidewalk to watch. St. Martin actually stopped his horse, took me gently out of my father's arms and hugged me. I will never forget how special that made me feel.

The recovery from the chicken pox is painfully slow and again leaves me vulnerable and weak during the winter months. My parents had intended to send me to high school the following spring, but on the advice of the teacher they wait another year for me to catch up all the time I have missed in school, so that I will be able to pass the entrance examination. When the day finally arrives for me to take the tests I am very nervous, yet confident that I will pass, and I do so with ease. During the examination something happens that is the talk of the larger town where the high school is located for weeks.

Apparently one of the students drew a Swastika from a line he was supposed to complete a picture with. Needless to say, he is disqualified immediately and I consider this to be extremely unfair. How could our parents' history, no matter how bad, ruin a child's dream of attending high school? But then there are many events during those early post-war days, which are not fair to those, who are likewise innocent victims.

A few weeks later my parents receive confirmation that I passed the entrance examination. That means the following spring I will be commuting on my bicycle for at least three miles each way attending a brand new high school. This is definitely one advantage being born shortly after the war, because every school I attend is located in a brand-new building.

That Christmas Eve, prior to my attending high school, my parents get married. My father has finally been able to obtain a divorce from his wife in East Germany and in a civil ceremony my parents become legally husband and wife. Actually my father has to adopt me in order to give me his name. At last I will not have to put up with three names any longer. This is a great relief for me.

After my father's death the actual Adoption Certificate is found among his papers. I was "bought" for 50 Marks, what a bargain!

Tante Grete and my Sisters

I don't know what I would do without Tante Grete at times. She adds so much to my life and since she is a widow never to remarry, she visits on most weekends. From afar I can see her walking along the path through the fields from the next village where she lives in a tiny apartment.

Sundays in Germany are terribly boring for children. There is Church in the morning and a big lunch, but then there is nothing to do other than on those days when Papa is home and it does not rain. Then we all get dressed up and after having cake and coffee we go for our Sunday afternoon walk through the woods, a tradition that is still carried out to this day.

Children are not allowed to go and play with their friends. No, this is family time, and so we walk through the woods in our Sunday best. In May this is truly fun because we go to the "Maikammer," where we spend hours picking big bunches of lily of the valley.

They grow in certain areas under the Oak trees and smell heavenly. We pick big bouquets and then finish them by surrounding the flowers with a skirt of leaves. They are taken home and the entire house smells of lily of the valley. Mama always puts some of them between the bed linen. The Rhineland tends to get a lot of rain and so more often than not I spend Sunday afternoons anxiously waiting for Tante Grete's arrival. She always brings the latest Mickey Mouse Comic Books, along with some magazines with the TV program for my parents. Meanwhile, since now we have electricity, Papa has splurged and purchased a television set. We only have one channel but it provides us with some entertainment. Papa likes to watch the news and sports. Once in a great while there is a good movie on, but the television screen is small and I could just as well do without it, especially since it further interferes with my sleeping. My bed is made up at night now in the living room on the sofa, which is as hard as a rock. I have to go to sleep early in my sister's bed. The walls are so thin that I can hear the TV and the family talking. Having trouble falling asleep and being a light sleeper this only aggravates my problem.

Once the others are ready to go to bed I am moved to my proper sleeping quarters. I am always moved about and that really upsets me. There is no space I can claim for my very own.

But Tante Grete's arrival is always anticipated eagerly, because while I have by now read myself through just about every book in the library of the elementary school, I have started to collect the Mickey Mouse Comic Books and love them. They make my Sundays special for years! Since I know Tante Grete purchases her magazines on Wednesdays one day I come up with the great idea to show up at Tante Grete's apartment when she returns from work, wanting to claim my Comic Book. But Tante Grete teaches me a lesson. She tells me I must wait until Sunday afternoon. She likes to read it herself first. I don't believe that because Tante Grete is an avid reader, even belongs to the Bertelsmann Book Club and has a ton of grown-up books, but she will not even let me have a peek. Instead she sends me home with a stern warning that some things one just has to wait for.

That day I learn an important lesson: waiting is worthwhile. Patience is not exactly the strong point of my slowly developing character but in time I will learn how essential patience is, in the way a life takes shape. So I walk back home through the fields while it is slowly getting dark and Tante Grete's stern admonition leaves a lasting impression.

There is another aspect of Tante Grete that makes her dear to me. She is independent and leads a very self-sufficient life. One of the things I learn from her is her love of working with her hands. She knits, crochets, and embroiders, all with absolute perfection.

Among others those are skills she teaches me and many a Christmas includes presents such as a good book as well as a craft project, eventually leading to my own love of knitting and embroidery. Tante Grete remains a steadfast influence on me. We share a lot of character traits and actually have more in common than my mother and I. After her death every time I visit my parents I go to her grave, plant a flower and spend a while reflecting on our close relationship. I never leave without telling her how much I love her and how much she added to my life.

The year prior to entering high school my sister becomes pregnant and at nine years of age I become an aunt myself. There is actually less of a span between my niece and me than between my oldest sister and me. All I remember is Mama disappearing for a private talk with my sister into her bedroom and both of them emerging with a smile announcing the good news. My sister is married and all is well. I am still totally ignorant of the facts of life, all I know is that my sister grows a huge belly and that one morning my brother-in-law shows up slightly tipsy, announcing that he is the proud father of a girl. He refers to her lovingly as "Sputnik" because her birth almost coincides with the first launch of the Russian satellite by that name. They move into a larger apartment and once in a while I go over to look at the baby, hoping my sister will ask me to stay for one of her delicious meals accompanied by potatoes in Bechamel sauce. I love the way she prepares them and it becomes a special treat. I do not have a particular fondness for babies though. As far as I am concerned they are too much trouble and cry too much. My sister's marriage is still going well at this point and her husband's drinking still tolerable.

Unfortunately he has to travel a lot since he works as a repairman on farm equipment.

They are a typical young German couple and my sister does not show any sign of illness.

As a matter of fact, she is fun-loving, outgoing and pretty plus an exemplary wife, housekeeper, mother and cook.

My other sister is dating the same boyfriend we met up with in the Black Forest while on vacation. My parents had not known that he would be joining us and their courtship is marred by the fact that his mother considers us "trash." His parents own a fine bakery in the next town and he is going to be an engineer. We are definitely a class below them and unworthy of their oldest son. His mother, a very outspoken and critical woman, who runs the lives of her husband and her three sons with an iron fist, is not happy with the situation. Quite often my sister, who now works as a secretary in Cologne, comes home in tears after being exposed to her future mother-in-law's sharp tongue and remarks about the fact that my mother had me, an illegitimate child, and that we live in a wooden shack. Nevertheless the courtship endures for many years. Yet again I feel the sting of hearing that I am a problem by my shear existence, something that is not easy to deal with when so young.

Inge Perreault

Entering High School

Finally the day arrives for me to enter high school and my mother purchases some new clothes as well as a new book bag for me. My father checks my bicycle to see that everything is in good working order, and I spend a long time shining the old trusty bike. From now on I will no longer be able to walk to school. I will have to leave the house by 7.15 in the morning on my bike in order to be at school in time. Classes begin at 8a.m. sharp.

The first day is cause for a sleepless night. I listen to the church bells strike every hour and count until it is time to get up. Not knowing anybody is something I am really not very comfortable with and it worries me a great deal. True, I have the proper name now and am no longer illegitimate, but everything is so very new. I know the way to the school and since this is the first day the new high school is opened, there is mayhem in the schoolyard. The bicycles have to be parked in the basement with a steep ramp leading down that is hard for me to manage. In the school yard the Principal holds a speech. Then we are called to line up according to our age group. Some of the older children have had to attend a high school further away, but since I am a new student I am in the first line to be called up and guided to the brand-new classroom.

Everything smells of fresh paint, the desks, chairs and blackboards are new and shiny.

Not much work is done the first day. According to German tradition students remain in one specific classroom all year, while the teachers for the different subjects move from class to class. Every class has a homeroom teacher, ours being my math teacher who happens to live in one of the new development homes not too far from my house.

Everything goes smoothly until the names are called taking attendance. Because my parents had not been married yet when I took the test for admission, the old name Windelschmidt still shows up on the list. When the name is called I do not answer. I want to silently slip away because the other children are laughing. They ·think it is a funny name. The teacher calls the name several times, then marks the person down as absent.

After the other children leave the room for a short recess I walk up to the teacher's desk teary-eyed and confess that the absent person is me. Choked by emotion I explain my situation to the teacher who is very kind and makes the required correction, but again, I feel worthless and different. The first day passes with the meeting of all our different teachers for the various subjects and the distribution of the study plan for the week, as well as a list of books and items we will need to purchase. I am glad when it is finally over. Dieter also goes to the same school but he is in a different class and so I am without a single friend.

Eventually I begin to make new friends, and we actually develop a system for the morning ride to school. Ursula picks me up first, then together we pick up another girl named Regina on the way. Until the end of high school the system stays in place. We have a good time riding together and talking. Occasionally we are reprimanded by a police officer, reminding us to ride in single file. It is much more fun to ride next to each other talking, and at this time the automobile traffic in Germany is not that busy yet.

The only thing I don't like about attending high school is the long ride, but eventually that as well becomes merely a routine, which after a while is actually enjoyable due to the companionship of my new friends. I am quite observant and enjoy certain things along the way I don't even share with the others. There is for instance an old farm house enclosed by a brick wall that we pass on our daily journey. One day I notice that there is a small birch tree growing on top of the brick wall and I follow its growth year after year, impressed by the tenacity with which the little tree reaches for light, stretches and takes its meager nourishment from the water trickling down the brick wall. Year by year it gets larger and every day during my years in high school my heart says "hello friend" to the little tree which grows against all odds. I feel a certain kinship. Like this tree I continue to grow in spite of all the obstacles which present themselves along the way.

I excel in the new school and am presented by our homeroom teacher with the book prize for best academic achievement at the end of the first school year, which makes me feel really good about myself. During this time my father and mother are busy with the completion of our new house and even though the relationship has temporarily quieted down, with the coming change again I succumb to anxiety and acute insomnia. Mother actually has a conference with the teacher and he recommends I be allowed to sleep in her bed on those nights when I cannot sleep. He feels this is a problem which eventually will resolve itself without medical attention. For a while it works and I sleep better.

During the spring of my second year in high school we make the actual move into the new house. It is wonderful; the most beautiful house on the street. Everything is new,

even the furniture in most rooms. My sister and I share a large bedroom in the rear of the house. I love waking up in the morning to birdsong and the smell of fresh paint, stretching comfortably for the first time in my very own bed under the crisp linen sheets.

Nevertheless, part of me misses the old homestead and quite often I walk quietly through the now empty rooms of what used to by my home. Humble as it was, still it sheltered me well for most of my childhood and part of me is left there. The memories are many, some very unpleasant and disturbing, yet there are others I don't mind recalling and am rather fond of. Now the old basement is used exclusively for the storage of potatoes, winter vegetables, fruit as well as coal, because even the new house is heated by coal stoves although there is a combination of a coal/electric stove in the new kitchen. During the summer months Mama no longer has to do her canning and juice-making on a hot stove, which made the process a much bigger chore than it is already. During the winter we can still enjoy the warmth of the coal kitchen stove and conserve energy. Papa has given great thought to energy conservation. His childhood experiences, the war and difficult post-war times are hard to shake off. Thus the bathroom is heated by the metal pipe which runs through the wall from the kitchen stove, the living room is only used and heated on weekends or holidays and the bedrooms are heated only when it is extremely cold.

That winter we all catch the flue and I remember all of us lying in bed for at least two weeks. The Doctor is summoned several times and brings us medicine. Mama is not even able to cook and so we exist on bread and marmalade we have on hand. Nobody feels like eating anyhow, we simply lie in our beds. All four of us simply wait to get better.

My oldest sister in the meantime has moved yet again, and sometimes I go to her apartment, located directly behind a Gaststaette (bar). That spring at Carnival, I find both her and her husband drunk to the point that I am worried about my little niece. I go home wondering about their situation and already then, at the age of 12, I know there is a serious problem. My sister stops drinking once her second child is born but her husband progresses to the point of being verbally and physically abusive. My sister does not deserve his treatment and after the birth of their third child, her war-experiences and the abuse from her husband will cause her to have a serious nervous breakdown from which she never quite recovers.

Meanwhile, during the summer of my first year in high school, my father suggests my mother and I take a trip to

East Germany to visit Uncle Otto, his oldest and favorite brother. Neither Mama nor I are very excited about going but we have a certain amount of free railroad tickets due to my father's employment with the Bundesbahn.

Unfortunately Papa can hardly ever take a vacation during the summer months when I have off from school. We decide to go, after all, it is something to do and a new experience. We set out from Cologne and change the border at Wolfsburg, the headquarters for the VW Works. I find it to be a rather unattractive industrial town.

Already from the West German side we can spot the border of barbed wire and the strategically placed watchtowers manned by armed soldiers. As young as I am, it strikes me as being extremely eerie. The border controls are very strict. We have to leave the train and the East German soldiers carefully check the train's washrooms as well as under the train. After a delay of about two hours we are finally allowed to leave and we enter a totally alien world. While in West Germany the rebuilding has taken place due to the Marshall Plan in a rather speedy fashion, in the East nothing has been done. Instead of tractors in the fields we see women with Russian-style headdress working with hoes and shovels. Every town we pass seems somehow decrepit, lifeless and run-down. The only sign of color are big posters plastered on every wall visible from the train with slogans such as: WE ARE FOR PEACE AND FREEDOM. It strikes me odd, since everyone looks very much afraid and not free at all. We distinguish ourselves from the East Germans simply due to our better quality of clothes, indicating that we are obviously visitors from the WEST, looked at with distinct suspicion and envy. Nobody talks to us.

Nobody even wants to sit next to us. I can tell Mama is very quiet and thinking, probably the same thoughts as mine! Finally we arrive at our destination and are picked up by our relatives, my father's brother and sister-in-law. They load our luggage on their bicycles and we have to walk a good hour before we reach their little village. There is no bus or taxi service. I like both, Uncle Otto and Tante Frieda. They are earthy honest people with good hearts and have two children of their own much older than me, my cousins Erich and Irma. Uncle Otto tells us right away that we must be more than careful in what we say in public. Their house is an old brick farmhouse and while they do own a television set which only shows old Russian war movies dubbed in German, they do not have outdoor plumbing and grow all their own food. Rationing coupons, long since a memory in West Germany, are still in force in East Germany. Going to the local supermarket, the HO, is astounding. I see nothing but empty shelves, a huge pickle barrel filled with pickles soaking in brine and some butter, which can be acquired with coupons.

Since West Germany is experiencing the beginnings of the Economic Miracle this is mind-boggling to a little girl. I truly feel like I am stepping back in time. My uncle gets milk from the goat he keeps, meat from the pig he raises every year and eggs from his chickens. He also keeps pigeons and for the first time in my life I get to taste a roasted pigeon with hardly any meat on it. My aunt bakes in an old brick oven and of course there is the obligatory outhouse. They do not even have regular toilet paper. Instead Tante Frieda cuts the newspapers into small sheets and the black print has a way of showing up in your under-ware. It feels as though I have been taken back to my very early childhood. I find the general atmosphere depressing since everything looks so run-down. The infrastructure, the roads and railways are badly in need of repair and I am surprised that nobody seems to care. We take a day-trip to the rather large town of Halle and visit a department store. Here again I am struck by the fact that other than some bolts of dull-looking coarse fabric and some handcrafted items, such as nutcrackers, the shelves are bare.. While Cologne has by now risen from the rubble and become a bustling reconstructed city, Halle bears the signs of the war like open scars.

Now and then we see some older women repairing the old cobblestone streets, work which in West Germany is definitely men's work. I notice the sullen expression on people's faces. They betray a despondent and hopeless feeling, yet at the same time I detect a certain animosity towards my mother and myself, since our clothes alone give away that we are "WESTERNERS."

On another occasion my mother takes me on a trip to Eisleben, the birthplace of Martin Luther and then a trip to a "Kolchose" (collective farm) outside of Eisleben. There my mother visits a friend she had made during the war years. A widow my mother's age, she lives in an attic under the eves of the old farm and has made a very cozy place for herself.

My mother asks her over a cup of coffee if she regrets having stayed in the East but this woman is beyond caring. Having lost everything and everyone in her family, her husband, children and other close relatives, she has settled into life on the collective farm, works a certain amount of hours each day and then retreats to her small private quarters wanting to be left to her own thoughts. There is no laughter or joy in this visit; both Mama and I come away with a deep feeling of sadness for her friend. Mama hardly says a word on the trip back and is deeply absorbed in

79

thought. I sit next to her quietly on the hard wooden benches of the pre-war train. Even the trains are old and decrepit.

My aunt and uncle have to work certain hours on the collective farm in their area.

Everything that is produced here ends up in Russia. That is why there is little enthusiasm on everybody's part. They also have to attend a political meeting twice a week whether they feel like it or not. It is the law. It seems they take Communism more seriously in East Germany than in Russia. Everybody is undergoing what almost amounts to brainwashing. As strange as it may sound, secretly my mother tells me that the most staunch supporters of Hitler are now the heads of the Communist Party in East Germany, a fact I cannot quite comprehend. Much later it becomes clear to me and I understand that those in power always have a way of rising to the top again, even if that entails a turn of 360 degrees.

Nevertheless I take some pleasant memories back from the area in which my father was born and raised. I love the animals, especially the goat at my uncle's house and I remember well walking through the forests of larch trees which are native to Saxony but I had never seen before. Apart from the garden around his own home Uncle Otto also leases a piece of property outside his small town. In Germany these plots are known as "Schrebergaerten." Here he grows more vegetables and there is a little tool-shed with a bench for resting on his plot. Sitting there I admire the largest red beech tree I have ever seen. It is huge and perfectly symmetrical, a gorgeous tree. When I ask my aunt Frieda about the tree's age, she tells me that it is said to having been planted when Napoleon occupied this area during his march on Moscow.

Upstairs in my uncle's house I discover in the attic an old gramophone, the type with a huge horn which you have to wind up, as well as a stack of old records.

There are also old fashioned dresses which I put on and dance all by myself to the sound of the old strange music. I even have a "Tea Party" all by myself.

Finally the day arrives for our return. We are all too happy to leave the oppressive atmosphere including the stupid huge billboards proclaiming East Germany stands for PEACE AND FREEDOM behind. The search at the border crossing back is twice as strict and I wonder while watching the soldiers searching for people who might want to escape, what type of government would proclaim to stand for peace and freedom, yet would not allow its people to move about freely in the world?

School resumes, and another year passes which is filled with studies, large amounts of homework and continued strife between my parents. Here and there a few weeks go by without a major clash of tempers but then it starts all over again. By now I simply cannot eat during the heat of the arguments that can last for days. I am sick quite often during that year, and other than the fact that now I have added to my income by selling excess fruit to some of my teachers in addition to my egg-route, I remember little that is worth mentioning.

I have made new friends. One of them is a pretty girl with long black hair named Ellen. She always wears the most beautiful outfits. Our friendship becomes very close and we visit each other quite frequently. She lives in an apartment with her parents and an older brother. Unfortunately her mother hears that we live in a beautiful new house with a large garden and she grows very envious.

One day my English teacher tells me to stay after class at the end of the school day, in order to advise me that Ellen's mother has been to see her, accusing me of copying her daughter's work. Confronted with this accusation I am speechless. As a matter of fact, it is me who has allowed Ellen to copy my work during exams when she did not know the answer. I tell the teacher and she believes me. However to prove her point I am informed that she will move me during class to another seat and that should reveal the truth. After the next two tests it becomes quite obvious that Ellen's mother was intentionally trying to hurt me with her accusations. I score substantially higher than Ellen in each test and the truth can be seen clearly. This marks the end of our friendship. Now, having bettered ourselves, not only me but also my parents become the victims of envious neighbors, since at this time our house is the most attractive one on the entire street.

How strange, I think, at first I am humiliated because of my illegitimacy and living in a shack, now envy is creeping into my life and makes it difficult. People are strange to say the least. I have a difficult time understanding the logic in this development.

That summer Mama and I travel to Hinterzarten in the Black Forest for three weeks.

I consider myself very fortunate. Due to the fact that each family member receives six free railroad tickets a year within Germany and 50% reductions for travel abroad, makes it possible for us to start traveling and having vacations. Everybody who knows Germany and Germans knows that they work very hard, but that they also like to travel.

Having six weeks vacation time is not unusual. Actually it is the standard vacation time given by most companies as well as to those who work for government institutions.

We stay at the same old farmhouse my sister and I visited before, enjoy wonderful hikes and lazy summer days. I have not forgotten how truly beautiful the Black Forest is, with the dense pine forests which give the region it's name. The fragrance of the pines in combination with the mossy trails is soothing to my mind and body. I feel well for once.

That fall in September my parents go on a three-week vacation to Italy. They have arranged for me to stay at a girl friend's house. Birgit's parents own a Laundry Business and we have a very nice time while my parents are away. Birgit is a single child and truly enjoys having company. Her parents are kind and I notice that this is a very peaceful household. We ride our bicycles to school together and I am almost sorry when my parents return. However, I feel Papa really needed a vacation. He works so hard not only at the railroad but also in his spare time as a painter and wallpaper hanger. In addition he takes care of the large gardens and the fruit trees. Mama too works hard, taking care of the flowerbeds, cooking, canning and all the other housework which needs to be done.

High school is fun for me. I continue to do well and receive the book prize for best achievements every year but one. The third year we have a different Math teacher who is a cranky old lady and does not like a pupil who questions her. During that year I go from an A to a C in math. We simply cannot connect but the following year I go back up to an A immediately. I never doubted my ability but it shows me the extent to which a teacher's personality can influence my performance and the resulting grade. Since the number of students in our grade has grown to such a large size that the classes are getting too big, the school decides to conduct an experiment and takes 50% of the students in the all male class who excel in languages and 50% of the student body in the all female class who excel in the sciences to be combined into a new "elite" class. The experiment turns out to be very successful and results in our class showing in general much better grades than the other classes, running concurrent with the same requirements. However, I like both, sciences as well as languages, and by now take English as well as French. My circle of friends widens and I become a member of the "in" group of smart students.

This is a time when hard working smart kids are not considered "nerds" but looked up to. The curriculum is very comprehensive with heavy emphasis on the sciences, languages, history and geography. None of the subjects are electives. Every student takes every subject on the curriculum including religious instructions. While sports is being taught twice a week all during my school years and there is an annual sports contest, we mostly concentrate on track and field during the summer months and gymnastics during the winter. For those who wish to join a soccer league they can, but that is done in their spare time on a municipal level. The funding of German schools comes from the Federal Government and the State level, thus leading to extremely low property taxes.

There is less emphasis on athletic achievements but much more on academic performance.

During history lessons we hear all about the terrible things the generation of our parents are responsible for, in particular the atrocities of the Holocaust, thus putting a heavy burden of guilt on us, their children. I remember many a heated discussion as we get older, because a lot of students do not feel they should carry the responsibility for events which occurred prior to their being born. Some of my fellow students are quite outspoken and the History teachers are at times backed into a corner they don't know how to deal with.

This is a tricky subject during these years and who can blame us. We were not even alive when these atrocities and injustices took place. Looking back the teachers merely did what they were instructed to do by the authorities, but for many of the sensitive students it leaves us with further guilt feelings and scars we really do not deserve.

There are annual school trips planned for each year. One year we go for a week to a camp in the Eiffel mountains, likewise there are day-trips such as Rhine-cruises including parents if they wish to participate. One memorable day-trip takes us to Amsterdam and the Reichsmuseum. There we spend the day admiring all the old masters. We are in particular impressed by Rembrandt's masterpiece "Die Nachtwache (the night watch)."

This particular trip is not only memorable in a positive fashion but also shows us how much Germans are still despised abroad. When we stop for lunch at a restaurant, we are refused service due to the fact that we are Germans. That is a heavy blow to children 12 years old and is very difficult for all of us to comprehend. The accompanying teachers try their best to explain the circumstances and reasons for the obvious animosity, but we feel we are being persecuted unjustly. After all, do two wrongs make one right? We are intelligent enough to understand that is not so. To us this action does not elevate the standing of the owners of this particular restaurant, as a matter of fact, to us they are no better than the Nazis who demanded Jewish citizens to wear a star on their clothes. A bunch of hungry and disillusioned schoolchildren return to Germany with dubious feelings about the wisdom of going abroad at this time. I am not one of them. I simply do not care. There is so much to discover in the world beyond German borders and while I did feel humiliated, I do not allow this incident to determine my future plans for exploring other countries and cultures.

West Germany is in the midst of a full recovery from the war years now and the old tradition of a family vacation is being revived. That summer we embark on such a vacation together for the first time. My father, mother and myself take a three-week holiday in Switzerland. The previous year my sister's future in-laws made a trip to the Italian part of Switzerland staying at the small village of Grono in the Swiss Italian Alps.

This is the first long train ride for me abroad and very exciting. Once we have passed the St. Gotthard tunnel and exit on the other side, I don't know which side of the train to look out of. The mountains are so very high, snowcapped and the sun is just setting on the very tops. It is so beautiful. A Swiss business man who has a daughter my age and is travelling in the same compartment talks to me and warns me to watch out for Vipers, poisonous snakes which tend to sun themselves on the rocks of mountain paths. Little does he realize that he spoils my fun to a great deal, since for the next three weeks I stomp around the mountain paths during our hikes, trying to make my presence known to the Vipers so they can slither away. We change trains at Domodossola and have to take another train running on smaller gauges to reach our final destination. One of the first impressions during my extensive travels that follow is usually the smell of a different place. In this case the night air is filled with a sweet unknown aroma which comes from the ripening grapes and figs grown in the area. By the time we finally arrive in Grono I am fast asleep and my father ends up carrying me part of the way. I am totally exhausted after the train ride of 16 hours. The village of Grono is small but very charming. We stay at a hotel which is part of a convent for retired members of the Catholic Church and run by nuns. The cost is very reasonable, the rooms comfortable and the food is very good. At first I am a bit lonely since there are no other children staying at the hotel. During the time my parents take a nap after lunch I am allowed to explore the village and make friends with some of the Italian-speaking Swiss children my age. Soon there is a group of us, Franca, Carmen, Georgio and a few younger ones playing together happily in the cobblestone streets of Grono. They teach me Italian, I teach them German, and we have a grand time together. During most days I take mountain hikes with my parents. There are huge waterfalls coming from the glaciers and sometimes it is so hot that we go to the little stream running along bottom of the valley to cool off. Glacier-fed the water is like ice but we are not

used to this heat and even a quick dunk helps us to cool off. Since we are not too far from Lugano and Locarno, beautiful tourist attractions along the shores of picturesque lakes, we make two day-trips to visit and this is probably the best time I have ever had with my parents. They are enjoying themselves while being relaxed and congenial towards each other. Why could it not always be like that I wonder? I am well behaved and thus able to explore the area with my friends without any restrictions. I wish we never had to leave. But the day comes when our lovely time ends and we have to board the train to go back home to dreary rainy weather, clouds that hang too low and school with lots of homework. Plus my parents revert to their normal pattern of resuming the explosive relationship that is theirs when we are at home. No wonder I did not want to return. I miss my new Swiss friends, the bright sunshine, the tall mountain peaks, the smell of olive and fig trees as well as the fragrant flowers. But most of all I miss and wish for a peaceful family life.

But that wish goes unfulfilled. By now I have resigned myself to this unpleasant fact of my life, in particular since for the moment I am not being drawn into any of the arguments. Mentally I try to remove myself and begin to spend a lot of time at the homes of various friends. One of them, Ute, has a father who subscribes to season tickets for the Cologne Opera house. During the next season I am invited to come along, since her mother cannot leave the ailing grandmother who lives with them. This is a real treat for me since my parents, other than while on vacation, never go out anywhere. Twice a year they go on a shopping trip for new clothes into Cologne, but Papa always complains of life and noise in the big city which give him a headache. He always will be a "country boy." Through Ute I get a priceless introduction into the world of theatre and opera. After the war the Opera House has found a new home in a brand-new modernistic building with a grand seating arrangement. My girlfriend's father is a great fan and thus we have really good seats. During the fall, winter and spring of that year I see a great variety of classics operas ranging from La Boheme to the Magic Flute. A new world opens itself to me and I develop a love for ballet. For months and months I practice by myself in the living room on my toes dancing to classical music and wish my parents had the money to send me to ballet classes. But they don't. There is a chubby girl in my class in school whose parents own a large furniture store and whose mother is sending her to ballet classes, naturally with the proper ballet shoes and a tutu. While it is not in my nature to be envious, in this case I make an exception. I would love to trade places with her, because I know I could do well. I have a good sense for combining music with movement, but for now it is a dream which remains unfulfilled; a dream that later I will revive in a different fashion and which will bring me lots of joy.

School continues and from year to year the book-bag I carry on my bicycle gets heavier and heavier. Unlike in America, in Germany children take their books home every day and on some days, especially on those when we have geography, requiring us to transport a heavy Atlas and enormously thick geography books, I am barely able to lift my bag and hoist it onto the bicycle carrier where it is strapped down. The demanding schedule leaves little time for socializing other than on weekends or during the brief vacations we have in the course of the year.

At home my parents have decided to have a central heating system installed. In order to pay for this large expense they have to sell half of our property. Somehow it feels odd to see another house go up on the land where my swing once stood and I could have an unobstructed view on clear days all the way to the Cologne Cathedral. But that is the price we have to pay in order not to have to stack coal brickets and deal with the disposal of coal-ash any longer. It also makes it possible to have hot water in the bathroom more than once a week for the traditional Saturday night family bath. My sister is still living at home although she has become formally engaged, and we are starting to become closer. We do share a bedroom and also share the bathroom mirror in the morning as she is getting ready for work and I for school. As I am growing older we talk more openly and as time passes we end up liking each other and confiding in one another.

The previous summer she had gone on vacation with her boyfriend to Austria, staying in a very small hamlet of a village in Tyrolia which can only be reached by Jeep from the next biggest town that has a railroad station. Her reports about the beauty of the mountains and the low cost of the guesthouse where they stayed, determine my next journey abroad. When the school year comes to the end and summer vacation begins, my mother, my father and I, set out for the Alps. I have done well in school and so I can go with a clear conscience knowing I have done my best. I look forward to long mountain hikes and fresh mountain air. It is a pity that Papa can only stay for five days and then has to return to work, but my mother and I will stay a total of three weeks.

By now I have become quite used to train travel and the huge locomotives, still powered by coal, do not intimidate me any longer. I bring good reading material for the boring part of the trip, although I always do look out of the window when the train on its way south follows the Rhine valley and passes through the mountainous area once we pass Koblenz. It seems as though nearly every other mountain top is graced with the ruins of a medieval castle and the terraced mountainsides are planted with pretty vineyards. Naturally all this pales in comparison once the Alps are reached, because it only takes about an hour to reach the really tall mountains from the area of the foothills. When we finally arrive at our destination we have to take the Jeep up to the tiny village of Ginzling, a hair-raising drive with switchbacks since the dirt road is only wide enough for the passage of one vehicle at a time. The village is charming, situated at the bottom of a high valley on both sides of a glacier-fed stream and consists of some farmhouses, two hotels with restaurants and a church. We stay at the lumber mill which during the summer season rents out rooms. To my great delight our room is located above the huge wheel, powered by the water of the stream and necessary to work the lumber mill. Being in this cozy room it sounds as though it is raining outside constantly, but the noise of the stream is soothing and the fresh mountain air, again heavy with the smell of pines and mosses but different from the scent I remember from the Black Forest, stimulates my appetite.

To me Austrians are strange people. I learned during my history classes that Hitler was a native Austrian, yet after the war was lost Austrians seem to have totally distanced themselves from him and his misdeeds, not taking any responsibility whatsoever. As a matter of fact, I can sense a dislike of Germans and feel it in the restaurants we frequent as well as when overhearing the conversations of the owners of the mill where we stay.

Somehow they seem to have forgotten that they too were part of the Third Reich and now envy the emerging economic prosperity in the new Germany. This seems odd to me because I notice that most tourists are indeed Germans and contribute a great deal to the Austrian economy as well as the financial wellbeing of the citizens in the small village where we are staying. But the feeling of not being liked due to the fact that we are German is very obvious and something I shall never get used to or approve of. How can you judge a person simply on the grounds of their country of origin, their color, race or religion? Even then I ask myself these questions and do not understand those, whose thinking is so limited and small that it does not allow them to just accept a person for who they are.

Nevertheless, staying at the mill in our little room with built-in furniture suspended over the raging river which drives the wheel is wonderful. When we are not out hiking the trails we spend time in our room because the owners actually make us feel uncomfortable in the common gathering room. They stop talking every time we enter. Mama and Papa have trouble with the attitude, being paying guests, but I really don't mind. I love to just look out of the window of our room and daydream.

Unfortunately the days Papa stays with us the weather is rainy and foggy, the mountain tops barely visible, but nevertheless we hike the trails to certain alpine huts, situated at the foot of various glaciers. We packed raingear and once in a while the clouds break open and allow a glimpse of a mountain peak. I love the alpine huts, not only because they provide a rustic cozy place to rest after a strenuous hike, but because of the hearty food and cider they serve. Usually there is only one item on the menu each day and that is what is served at a very reasonable price. The wives of the farmers living in the alpine huts during the summer months, when the cattle is allowed to graze way up high on the meadows, are usually excellent cooks and prepare a hearty meal. People from different parts of Europe sit around crude tables and engage in lively conversations.

After my father leaves to go back to work my mother and I enjoy two weeks of glorious weather. We continue hiking the well-marked trails and even take a two-day hike together with another young woman who is travelling alone. During the entire vacation this is the greatest experience. It takes an entire day to reach our goal, an alpine hut named Alpenrose way above the tree line. On the way there we stop at another one for lunch, and once above the tree line we find a profusion of native flowers such as Edelweis and Alpenrosen. There are some rather scary areas we have to pass through since the trail leads right along the edge of the mountains, but we are careful and finally make it just when the last sun-rays are setting behind the glacier which the Alpenrose looks out on. The night gets cold this high up, even in July, and we welcome our beds made up with fresh crisp linen sheets and huge featherbeds. The next morning, after a hearty breakfast, we set out early to climb even higher. There we rest a while by a lake rimmed with snow. I actually throw snowballs into the icy blue, frigid waters which are crystal clear and then we get ready for the descent back to Ginzling.

The town, being a high valley, never gets any sunshine. This is one reason I would not like to live there on a permanent basis. The valley is so narrow that the sun does not reach to the very bottom and so the people who live there must hike a while upwards if they wish to catch a ray of sun. Personally I do not think I would care to live without sun reaching my house or garden. The area I come from is flat as a tabletop and though it rains so very often, when the sun does shine there is no obstruction to the sun's rays reaching into every nook and cranny. This vacation leaves me with powerful memories of natures wonders and from then on I read the book "Heidi" over and over again.

I can just imagine how wonderfully cozy grandfather's hut in the high mountains must have been and how, having to live in a big city, Heidi's health and spirit suffered while she longed for her beloved grandpa and those mountains. In any given chapter I can put myself right into the book and feel what Heidi must have felt: the peace, the tranquility and the serenity of being in such close touch with nature.

Austria

When getting ready for the return trip to Cologne neither one of us is in the mood for a flat landscape and the constant rain and dampness of the Rhineland, but that is where we live and so we return home and life goes on.

I return to school, get to know my new teachers for the year and resume my studies which are getting more difficult from year to year. My friends remain the same and once again I do very well in my schoolwork even though, that winter, once again I get sick quite often and miss out on many school days. There is something wrong with my thyroid and I am undergoing iodine treatments which leave an ugly stain on my neck. Nevertheless, I still struggle on a constant basis with my health.

The Tonsillectomy

The spring in which I celebrate my 13th birthday, my mother drags me from doctor to doctor, to homeopaths and irodologists, but nobody knows what is wrong me. Finally they decide it must be my tonsils. They are big and swollen, apparently not doing their job of filtering out bacteria any longer. So my mother takes me to Dr. Winter, who took out hers' and those of my oldest sister. I remember them talking about it and how both of them screamed bloody murder. Dr. Winter has a reputation for being tough and his nickname, unbeknownst to him, is "The Horse Doctor." Naturally, I go there with great trepidation. My mother takes me and I sit in his office, facing this formidable man who determines when I have to check into the hospital.

Yes, my tonsils indeed need to come out.

It is the same hospital where I was born and is run by Catholic Nuns, likewise the Carmelites. I am no longer afraid of their odd headdress, but they too have a reputation for being tough.

On the day of the surgery my mother takes me there early in the morning.

I am asked to undress, put on a surgical gown and sit in a chair in the middle of this cold, sterile room that reminds me of the pictures I have seen of electric chairs on television: the type they have in America where they execute people. The nurse proceeds to strap me down with leather straps and fear begins to set in.

By now I am not "chicken" about physical pain, but suddenly it hits me: this is going to hurt! The doctor walks in, very tall, very official looking. He wears his white coat, and his stethoscope is hanging around his neck. He is a rather sullen man; a no nonsense kind of person. Sitting down on a stool on rollers in front of me, he asks me to open my mouth wide, then proceeds to give me nine novocaine injections into the back of my throat. "I'll be back in twenty minutes, after my morning rounds," he says, then leaves me strapped down alone in this terrible room. As the novocaine begins to take effect I focus on the door ahead of me, through which the Horse Doctor disappeared, a gray metal door that looks like a prison door. Letting my eyes wander over the room, I detect all kinds of evil looking instruments and determine in my mind that this looks like a "torture chamber." There is nothing cheerful that could catch my attention. After what seems like an eternity the door opens and Dr. Winter is back in his imposing "tallness" and no-nonsense "I am here to do a job" manner.

He pulls up the little stool on rollers, places a metal container into my hands, which I can barely hold due to being strapped into the chair, and I wonder what it is for. I find out as soon as he tells me to open my mouth and starts to cut away at my tonsils: it is there to catch the blood that is flowing freely from my mouth. I look straight ahead at the doctor's face while he is cutting in a very determined manner. Although I don't feel anything, I can hear the sound of him cutting my flesh and it sounds awful. Before I know it, there is one huge tonsil laying in a steel dish, a piece of putrid looking flesh that I find hard to believe was part of me. The blood is starting to flow more quickly now and some is running down my windpipe making me cough. All of a sudden the doctor in front of me in his snow-white coat is splattered in red and he curses. I want to tell him I am sorry but I cannot close my mouth because some weird instrument is clamped into my other tonsil. He yells at me for coughing and making him look like a butcher but I cannot help it. To his great annoyance I have to cough again. When he is finished cutting out the other tonsil, equally big and putrid looking which he places in the bowl, he calls the nurse and without giving me a further look, tells her to take me to my room.

'The nurse removes the straps that held me tied to the chair and takes me by my arm. I walk like in a trance being guided to the elevator. It comes to a halt and we step in. There is a woman in her 50s lying on a stretcher.

As she takes a look at me her eyes get extraordinarily wide and she proceeds to utter "My God, oh my God." I am just standing there looking at her and wonder why she keeps saying that over and over again, but the door opens and the nurse guides me to my room. As I walk by the mirror over the sink I realize why the woman on the stretcher kept saying "Oh my God." My face as well as the front of my gown are soaked in blood but I don't care. I am still numb. The room contains two beds, one occupied by a young girl about 17 or 18 years old and one bed for me. The nurse helps me into a fresh night-gown, puts me to bed, and about 30 minutes later comes back with an ice-pack for my neck. The novocaine is beginning to wear off and it begins to hurt, really bad. I have promised myself not to be a whiner, so I suffer quietly, slipping in and out of a dream-like state.

For the rest of the afternoon nobody comes to check on me. Eventually the mother of my roommate shows up for a visit. Taking one look at me she leaves the room and I hear her talking rather harshly to the head nun of the ward. She returns with a fresh ice-pack replacing the one that by now is body temperature, places it compassionately on my neck and proceeds to straighten out the covers of my bed as well as fluff my pillow. While doing so, she is making comments about the lack of compassion on the part of the nursing staff and Catholic Nuns in particular. I just look up at her with grateful eyes. By now I am in great pain but there is no pain medicine coming forth. The nurse comes in once prior to shutting off the lights at night and takes my temperature. Apparently I am running a slight fever which is considered normal. During the night I drift off on occasion into a restless sleep and eventually watch the sun come up, watery looking as it is at this time of spring in Germany.

It hurts, terribly, but I bear it with a certain stoicism. Even though I feel awful I am getting hungry. I have not eaten or had anything to drink in over 24 hours, and finally the nun appears, headdress and all, with my breakfast.

I cannot believe my eyes. There is a cup of coffee and a slice of rather dry-looking rye bread with liverwurst cut into small cubes in front of me. I can barely swallow my own saliva and I am supposed to eat that?

It feels like swallowing glass shards but I am hungry and so I force down a few pieces. Around noon my mother comes to visit me. It is hard to talk; as a matter of fact, I can barely whisper. She sits by my bedside in the detached manner that is her habit when I am sick. I never quite know what she is thinking or if she feels sorry for me. She is a difficult person to figure out.

My father on the other hand is a born nurturer and very caring when I am ill, but he cannot come to visit me because he is on day shift this week and has to work. Visiting hours are from 12p.m to 5 p.m. My mother has brought me some grilled chicken and I tear off little pieces of soft meat and swallow it with great difficulty. There is still no pain medication and there will be none.

I like the girl who is my roommate. She is about 17 and had her surgery a few days ago. While she realizes that I cannot talk, she makes me laugh and helps me wash up in the morning. The nuns don't do much other than stick their heads in a couple of times a day. I will be there for a full week without having my bed made once. My roommate receives a big bouquet of roses from her boyfriend and is thrilled. I receive a bouquet of carnations from an "anonymous" admirer, the type of crush a boy has at 13 or 14 and find out eventually that they are not from whom I thought they were. But that's o.k., at least it makes me feel wanted.

The next morning I start to come around a bit. Looking out of the window my roommate and I see smoke coming out of a certain part of the hospital complex. She jokes that they are probably burning body parts including our tonsils, and we giggle imagining them going up in smoke.

That day her mother visits and brings her a big box of chocolates, which she shares with me freely. At night, before the light is shut off, a nun comes into the room to check on us, and my roommate offers her a piece of chocolate. To our great surprise she takes the entire box, says "thank you," and disappears, leaving us speechless. So much for charity; my roommate plots revenge. Unfortunately she is released the next day and I miss her dreadfully. Even the book I am reading cannot make the pain in my throat go away, and I am glad when the day comes for my mother to pick me up. According to doctor's orders I have another week of bed rest ahead of me and then, prior to being allowed to go back to school, I have to see the "Horse Doctor" for a final check-up.

This day we find him in a better mood than usual. I am relieved to see him in a better frame of mind than during the operation. He checks my throat, declares it to be looking well and gives me the o.k. to return to school. My mother pays him in cash and he takes a bill of 10 DM, hands it back to my mother and says: "Give this to your daughter. I have never had a patient who has not screamed bloody murder." (Let's not forget he also operated on my mother and my oldest sister) "She was an excellent patient, she deserves to be rewarded." Then he smiles at me and at that very moment I change my mind about Dr. Winter, not because of the money, but because of what he said. Finally someone realized that under all my weakness there is a tough core. I think he is the first person to ever notice that. While the tonsillectomy was not a pleasant experience by far, I come away from it with a certain feeling of pride; of having been brave and withstood pain without whining or complaining. My mother gives me the money on the bus ride back home but she does not make any comment.

Secretly I think she probably feels bad for having screamed bloody murder herself during the same surgery. But then again, my mother is a difficult person to figure out.

High School Continued

I return to school pale and sickly looking from the ordeal. Since spring vacation is approaching, Mama decides to take me out of school an extra week, in order for her to take me on a trip to Italy, where she and my father have been before, allowing me to recuperate fully. By now it has become quite obvious that the other children as well as some of the teachers are becoming envious of my travel opportunities, but if it were not for my parents' thrift and my father's free and reduced railway tickets, we would never be able to afford the amount of travel we do.

Sometimes I think Mama just wants to get away from Papa, because they fight regularly about my older sisters or about things that happened many years ago.

I will never understand how a person can allow these really unimportant things to spoil the present. Therefore I avoid the house on those occasions deliberately and ask permission to stay over at a girl-friend's home. Permission is usually granted and I try to forget what a dysfunctional household I come from. My girl-friends and I study together, do our homework and take long bike rides. Then at night we read or talk about the things 13 year old girls talk about: boys, clothes and future dating.

My French teacher, whom all the girls adore because he is handsome and quite charming, particularly makes a big issue out of the fact that I will take an extra week off to go to Italy. I find his comments a bit embarrassing because normally I am one of his favorite students; but after all, he is only human. He probably would like to go himself. Since I am doing well in all my classes my mother is not worried, as a matter of fact, I do not once remember having been asked whether I have done my homework or trying to hide a test result from my parents, since I always do what is expected of me.

By now I have become a typical overachiever. That has become part of me as much as trying not to cause any trouble at home whatsoever, because the things that were said when I was very little left such lasting and deep wounds. I internalized them deeply.

I even tell my parents when I get into trouble, such as when I allow my best friend to copy the results of a math test she does not know, get caught and am punished by the math teacher, who angrily slaps the math book right in my face. This is extremely unfair in my mind, because my friend gets away without any punishment and it was she who wanted to copy the results. The embarrassment hurts more than being hit by the thick math book, nevertheless my conscience dictates that I tell my parents. I am reprimanded, because in those days the teacher always does the right thing and his authority is not undermined or even questioned by a parent.

Once the spring vacation starts, Mama and I set out by train for Italy. I very much look forward to crossing the Alps and seeing the Mediterranean. Actually I will be seeing an ocean for the very first time. Mama has told me that it is very beautiful and that there are even palm trees along the main promenade, but I am very curious to see these things for myself. Other children my age have more toys, clothes or are allowed to go to ballet lessons, but I get to travel and the Tumbleweed character grows and stretches inside me. Somehow I know deep in my heart that I am preparing to break away some day in the future when I reach maturity. It is fun to dream, allowing myself to get carried away by the wind. I do not realize that it will be a storm that will cause me to give in to my longing, but the foundation is being laid unbeknownst to my parents.

Papa takes us and the luggage to the main station in Cologne, where we catch the train to Ventimiglia; and since the journey starts in the early evening, getting us to our destination not until the following day around 1p.m., my parents booked a sleeper car.

Thus we get to sleep comfortably while we begin crossing Germany. By the time we enter the Gotthard Tunnel, which enters on the Swiss German side and exits on the Italian side of Switzerland, the first rays of sunshine hit the high mountain peaks and I cannot get enough of the vistas moving by the window. At each border crossing we have to show our passports and at each station I open up the window wide to take in the foreign smell of a new place. I am in my glory! My heart pounds the first time I catch a glimpse of the sky-blue Mediterranean. Along the coast the train winds at times precariously close to the ocean, and I am surprised by the combination and sweet beauty of green mountains falling quite abruptly into the sea.

At our destination we take a taxi and get to the hotel where we are staying. It is merely a minute walk from the beach, and even though in May the water is still quite chilly, I like swimming and resting in my beach chair while looking out over the endless blue ocean and sky. I love the feeling of being in a foreign country and get to use the little Italian I learned when in the Italian part of Switzerland. We visit the local market where everything from fresh fish to beautiful jewelry and clothes can be purchased. One must haggle with the vendors because, unlike in Germany, the prices are not fixed. My mother makes some new friends and sometimes we go out together at night, along the main promenade graced on each side by beautiful palm trees.

Some ingenious individual has had the idea to plant colorful hanging geraniums right into the part of the palm trees where the leaves fan out, and with lights shining from the ground into the trees it makes for a stunning visual effect. I have never seen such palm trees or flowers like these and admire them greatly. My love for nature, instilled in me during those early years, continues to grow. Whenever I am troubled, that is what buoys me up; on the other hand when I am happy, this love of all living things just serves to increase the happiness I feel.

One morning we rise early, very early, to meet the fishermen at the beach when they unload the fish they caught during the night from their boats. Usually they give the tourists little seahorses or starfish as souvenirs .That morning I remember feeling odd and dizzy. I try to tell my mother I don't feel well but she brushes me off, telling me to just sit down somewhere while she is looking for seahorses. The next thing I remember is waking up and lying on the beach while a young lady, a medical student, is bringing me back to consciousness. A big crowd of people is surrounding me. The medical student asks where my mother is, but she is nowhere to be found until, all of a sudden, her curious face is peeking through the crowd, wondering what the special catch of the fishermen might be. Then I can hear her yelling: "Mein Gott, das ist doch meine Tochter!" (My God, that is my daughter), and she quickly makes her way through the dense crowd coming to my rescue. By now I am fully conscious but confused about what happened. I know I feel intense panic but I do not understand why, and actually, I have not fainted in quite a while. The rest of the day I am told to stay out of the sun and rest quietly. Afterwards, when thinking about what happened, it somehow strikes me almost funny seeing my mother's face peeking curiously through the crowd. She is a rather short woman and must have been standing on her toes to catch a glimpse of the catch of the day – ME!

The two weeks pass much too quickly. All too soon we have to leave and go back to the humdrum life of schoolwork, homework, duties in the garden and helping out around the house. My oldest sister has moved away to another town by now and I miss her and the baby a lot. My other sister is still engaged to the same young man, waiting for him to finish his studies so they can get married. I do not go on a vacation that summer since I already had a vacation. But my parents go and leave me in the care of my older sister that September. After school I stop off for a hot lunch at the house of one of my parents' friends and my sister takes care of dinner. I do not mind having the house all to myself during the hours my sister is not home, although I do remember checking under the beds to make sure I am the only person in the house. Television shows have begun to influence the mind of youngsters, especially the ones dealing with crime. So I check wherever someone could hide, such as under the beds, in the closets and definitely the basement. Only after I have convinced myself that there is nobody else in the house who wants to harm me do I feel comfortable. It is also my duty to collect the eggs and put the chickens into the coop at night. My parents return from Italy well rested and very tanned. At the age of 50 my father has actually learned how to swim. I think that is amazing. Having learned to swim myself only the year before, I am very proud of him.

He never had the chance to swim when he was a child, and a simple accomplishment such as that makes him extremely happy. I myself learned how to swim the previous summer. All my friends knew how to swim already, and I was tired of being confined to the area marked for "Non-Swimmers." As a matter of fact, my friends were jumping off the diving boards and dared me to jump from the three meter one. So I simply asked the best swimmers to be in the area, climbed up to the diving board and jumped with tightly closed eyes and clenched fists. My friends were supposed to grab me and pull me to the side of the public pool, but once I came up to the surface, I was miraculously able to swim. I told them to stay away and swam all by myself to the edge, climbed back up the three meters board and jumped again, all afternoon until I had to go home. I won the dare that day and the respect of my friends as well.

Toward the beginning of October, not too long after my parents' return from Italy, we take a class trip for a week to the Island of Langeoog in the North Sea. We are being supervised by our English teacher, History teacher and Music teacher, the latter a young woman in her early 30s. Seeing the North Sea after having seen the Mediterranean is very anti-climatic. However, quite a few of my fellow students have never seen the ocean. It smells totally different, I notice, and I marvel at how far the tide goes out since we arrive by train and have to wait for four hours until the boat can leave to take us to Langeoog. There is simply no water in sight when we arrive, nothing but what is called in German the "Wattenmeer," the exposed bottom of the ocean and people digging for clams or looking for stranded starfish. Then, at the appropriate time, the water returns rushing in like a flood, and it is an astounding natural phenomenon to watch. The boat, just minutes ago was stranded on solid ground lying precariously on its side, is now floating upright and ready to board. Unlike the Mediterranean, the North Sea is steel gray in color and foreboding looking. Heavy clouds are hanging even lower than they do at home in the Rhineland but I decide not to compare this experience with another and take from it whatever it has to offer. By now I have learned that there is beauty to be found in all different forms of nature.

The trip by boat is smooth. We are picked up at the docks with several wagons for our luggage, which we pull by hand along the paths leading through high dunes to the Youth Hostel where we are going to spend a week. From our windows upstairs we can look out over the dark and menacing-looking North Sea over the dunes which protect the small cluster of homes as well as hotels, built in the typical style of Northern Germany, with thatched roofs reaching very low to the ground.

The days are spent hiking through the dunes and along the shoreline. By now it is much too cool for swimming in the rough northern seas. The waves are pounding the wide beaches and the wind is so strong that we have to hold on to our raingear. Yet, there certainly is beauty to be found on this northern vacation island during the off-season period. I like to watch the frothy waves come ashore, sitting with my friends in the protection of the large dunes, with the beach grass blowing about and the sun peeking out ever so often from behind the dark clouds. It is a different kind of beauty than that of the Mediterranean, but beauty nonetheless. While a few hours every day are spent in the Youth Hostel learning about the area and its history, we have a lot of fun with bonfires at night in the dunes.

One day we build a human pyramid with me on the top since I am very thin and light. When the pyramid collapses I am caught by the boys who formed the bottom of the pyramid, accompanied by a lot of laughter. The food is the only thing everyone is complaining about. Almost every day we are served a type of stew with meat so tough that all of us sit in the dining room looking at one another chewing like cows. The boys proclaim they are certain it must be horsemeat, and most of it ends up in our napkins or back on the dinner plates. The entire school trip is a great success though, and we return home with many happy memories. Discipline has been strict but not excessively so.

Everybody has done what was expected of him or her.

Regular school resumes and with that tons of homework. For me life at home continues in the fashion I have become used to and ever so often there are even times when my parents get along with a minimum of bickering and fighting.

That particular year our French teacher is also our History teacher. The guilt is piled heavily on us German youngsters, the immediate post-war generation. We hear about all the misdeeds and atrocities which occurred under Hitler. Sometimes there are heated debates because some of the students have received a different message from their parents and often the History teacher finds himself in a great quandary and much frustration. The same scenario is beginning to play itself out during religious instructions, because we have just entered our teens and like to question everything. It is not done in an effort to annoy the teachers and free discussion is encouraged, however some of the students push a bit too far sometimes, which leads to either a parent-teacher conference or a reprimand from the School Principal. I like most of my teachers; however, there are some whose teaching methods could be marketed as a "sleep-aid." It is actually difficult to stay awake during their classes.

The year goes by in a flash. Christmas comes, and this particular year is made special by the presence of a little bird. That fall I found an injured German Robin Redbreast, very different from the American robins and about the size of a wren. Mama put a splint on the little creature's broken leg, and since it could not migrate, we have been keeping it in the basement, a daylight basement, where it can roam about freely. Every day after school I have gone down there to feed and play with my little feathered friend.

Eventually the bird becomes so tame that it will perch on my finger. On Christmas Eve with the Christmas tree standing in a corner of the living room in its full glory, my father suggests we allow the bird to come upstairs and sit in the tree. I am the one who goes to fetch it and release it in the living room. As soon as it spots the Christmas tree it flies toward it and perching on the highest branches begins to sing his heart out. All of us feel inspired by the presence of this little songbird whose life we were able to save.

The following spring we release it back out into the yard, once the migrating birds have returned. This is one of the few Christmases that I remember with special fondness, not because of the presents that were exchanged, but because of the song of a little wild bird giving an extraordinary Christmas concert to a very private audience.

Next come Carnival, Lent and Easter. The Rhineland, especially Cologne, is renowned for the elaborate and extensive celebration of the pre-lenten Carnival season, which officially begins on the 11th day of the 11th month of every year and culminates in Rosenmontag, Shrovemonday, with a huge parade starting from the Cologne Cathedral winding its way through the main streets of the city. Big floats are constructed according to the chosen theme of the year, and children dressed in silly costumes love to catch the candy that is thrown from the floats by the armload. The key of the city is ceremoniously handed over by the city's mayor to Price Carnival each year until, on Ash

Wednesday, the festivities come to an end, usually leaving in its wake a lot of people nursing hangovers from the copious amounts of liquor they have consumed during the previous week.

The tradition has its roots in pagan beliefs and goes back hundreds of years. Each year the citizens of the Rhineland look forward to these events with great anticipation. To my knowledge, the only years it did not take place, were the war years during the first and second World Wars. My mother, being a native of Cologne, loves Carnival and the parades. Now that I am older she takes me with her, but my father, coming from Protestant Saxony, does not share the same sense of humor and gets no enjoyment from these activities. He usually stays home and works. Since he does not like to drink, other than a glass of beer on rare occasions, he has little sympathy for his co-workers who are nursing hangovers. Every year he gets annoyed with them. Mama considers him a real "stick in the mud" and I guess one must have grown up with the tradition, in order to feel totally uninhibited and joyful. This pagan ritual has been adapted to fit into the Catholic season of lent, and I understand that as late as the beginning of the 19th century adultery, committed during Carnival, was not considered grounds for divorce. That has since changed, and I am aware of many broken marriages due to acts of infidelity occurring during the Carnival season.

The school year ends just prior to summer vacation, and once again I receive the book prize for best achievements during the year. The little birch tree I have been passing daily on my way to school is getting rather tall, and I am constantly amazed at how tenaciously this tree clings to life, managing to grow on top of a brick wall. There is a good lesson in that, showing me the importance of persistence and tenacity, yet another lesson I take from my love of nature, which in the future will help me over many a hurdle in life.

That year my parents plan to return for a vacation in September to the Italian Riviera, and there is not enough money for my mother to take me on a separate vacation. However, the parents of my girl-friend Birgit are planning a trip to the Austrian Alps, and they are willing to take me along as a companion for their daughter. All my parents have to pay for is my share of the hotel room and my meals. This is my first trip to the Alps by car and gives me a totally new perspective. We visit a different valley in the high mountains, the Oetztal, named for the little river which runs along the bottom of the valley. The village is quaint and charming. Again we stay at a farmhouse renting out rooms for the summer season. Having a car gives us more mobility and we get to travel about more than we actually hike, but being with a friend from school my own age is a lot of fun. I am really grateful that I did not have to stay home the entire summer, and the fresh mountain air is invigorating. I don't think either one of us, Birgit or I, will ever forget the time we spent together that summer. Especially not the joke her uncle pulled on us by hiding in the closet of our room, suddenly jumping out and scaring us half to death.

When school resumes that fall, two new subjects are added to our already heavy curriculum: physics and chemistry. The school days are getting longer with an increasingly demanding curriculum and ever increasing homework. While I absolutely love physics, chemistry will forever remain a mystery to me. I memorize whatever I have to, but to this day I have a mental block where chemistry is concerned. I continue excelling in the other subjects, especially the languages, mathematics, history and geography. While until now I have never enjoyed German very much, our new teacher, Frau Dorau, is inspiring. She is a woman who to this day has my full respect for her extreme sense of fairness, even though she is very demanding and a strict disciplinarian.

I begin to enjoy writing compositions on subjects such as the interpretation of certain works of art. At one time we are asked to present a composition of one of Duerer's most famous paintings, three women of different ages kneeling in a church pew praying. I take the approach of interpreting the meaning of the painting by focussing on the hands. Frau Dorau gives me the best grade, and I even have to read the composition aloud in front of the class. That has never happened before. This excellent teacher just exudes confidence and integrity. Later on she becomes the Principal of another High School, a promotion that is very well deserved. There is nobody who would even think of not taking this wonderful teacher seriously or of intentionally annoying her. She really knows how to bring out the best in every student because you really don't want to disappoint her.

Carrying a full load I nevertheless take on my first "job." I am hired by the future mother-in-law of my sister to help out on Sunday afternoons selling cake and other delicacies at their bakery. While I still have my egg-route and sell excess fruit to several people in town, now I get paid by the hour and as a special bonus I can choose one piece of cake or Torte each week to relish during my 15 minute break. Since the bakery is a "Konditorei," specializing in cream cakes and fine bakery goods, it is a difficult choice each week but oh, what a sweet choice. Never before have I seen or tasted cream cakes as high and rich as these. The future father-in-law of my sister rises at two o'clock in the morning and with the finest ingredients prepares sheer ambrosia. His Schwarzwaelder-Kirschtorte, Eissplittertorte and others are beyond compare. Naturally it also makes me feel very adult to stand behind the counter, to take an order, then assemble the required bakery goods and wrap them properly, accept payment and render the proper change. It takes me 30 minutes by bus to get to and from the bakery, but my income is greatly enhanced and ever so often I can spend money on something my parents would not pay for under normal circumstances. These are the days before "allowances" become the norm, and while having to earn one's own money is difficult with the heavy work-load at school, it is also a good lesson in thrift and in making a choice what to spend one's hard-earned money on.

That Christmas I am allowed to wear my first pair of nylon stockings and a pair of high-heeled shoes. Tiny as they may be, the heel is there and I fit in with all the other budding teenagers. The "petticoat" period has come and gone, the next step to adulthood will be wearing a tight skirt, something I eagerly look forward to. My sister is still living at home and without her knowing, ever so often I try on some of her clothes.

In the mornings we still share the mirror in the bathroom, getting ready at the same time while she answers the many questions I have regarding the changes I experience in my body as well as "BOYS." These are things I cannot talk to my mother about. I just don't feel comfortable doing so and am glad to be able to draw on the knowledge of an older sister. In general I am happy with my appearance although according to my sister I have "Gibbon arms." There is one part though I am extremely unhappy with and that is my smile, since my teeth are rather crooked.

They are strong and healthy teeth but have earned me the nickname "Vampire" or "Dracula."

Braces are not something my parents would pay for, as a matter of fact uneven teeth are quite a common sight in post-war Germany. So I try to adjust my smile and pictures of me never show my teeth. I am just too embarrassed.

Either I did not go for a summer vacation the following summer or I don't remember, most likely though it is the summer my mother had her gallbladder removed and my help was needed at home.

The year prior to graduating from high school our class takes an eight-day long journey by boat through the canals of Holland, stopping off in all the important towns along the way. Although the accommodations on the boat are tight, 6 to a room sleeping on triple-bunks, a great time is had by all. Our English teacher and our Music teacher arranged the trip and we visit the porcelain factories of Delft, spend lots of time on deck looking at windmills while singing along with the guitar play of the Music teacher, and every night we dock in a different town. By now the Dutch are more congenial towards Germans and no longer quite as prejudiced as during our previous trip. We enjoy visiting The Hague, Rotterdam and especially Amsterdam. It just so happens that another boat full of exclusively male high school seniors from Leverkusen takes the same route and nightly we dock next to each other. Eventually we are allowed to socialize under the strict supervision of the teachers. Some of us make friends, exchange addresses and later correspond with each other.

I correspond with a young man nick-named Ginger because he has red hair, and when that September my parents go on their by now annual vacation to Italy, I receive permission from my mother to give a small party at my house, as long as my sister is present. An invitation goes out to the friends we made on our trip and on the prearranged Saturday my sister goes on a date while four friends and I wait anxiously for the arrival of our invited guests. As 8 o'clock approaches, a mass of vehicles descends on my street, taking up every single parking spot. Kegs of beer are carried into the house, and before I know what is happening, the living room furniture is being carried upstairs and the Oriental rug rolled up, creating a dance floor. There are so many young men, some we don't even know, that I am absolutely petrified and pray my parents will never find out. Actually, apart from the fact that one of them throws up all over our garbage can due to excessive drinking, nothing is damaged but I really do not enjoy this party. My friends and I are in way over our young heads. I am actually relieved when everybody goes home and try to explain to my sister that I had no idea so many people were going to show up bringing along alcoholic beverages. She surveys the damage, determines it is not too bad and helps me rearrange the living room furniture. But it is I who has to clean up the vomit covering the garbage can, something so disgusting that I swear off having any further parties at my house.

The following year I am enrolled in a Dancing School. This is basically designed not merely to teach us ball-room dancing but it is also a finishing school, teaching us proper manners when socializing. The lessons take place twice a week for the duration of six months, including a mid-term ball and a big final ball with a dance competition as the crowning end. My friends from high school and I meet at the trolley stop in the suburb, from where we go on together to the Dancing School located in the center of Cologne.

These are fun-filled days, and while I am still haunted by anxiety, it is manageable because a lot of pleasant and exciting things are happening in my life. At home, for the time being, a point of relatively peaceful coexistence is taking place. While I was denied the chance of ballet lessons earlier, now I have the chance to combine my sense of body rhythm with music, and dancing develops into a passion that will carry me through the next four years. Mama buys me a new dress for the mid-term ball, dark blue with a low-cut back that is the fashion then, and another ball-room gown for the final ball and dance contest. It is pink and feels like I am wearing a cloud. With it come the matching shoes and fancy gloves reaching up to my elbows. While my mother is not an outwardly affectionate person, she delights in dressing me up now and showing me off. In a strange way I feel that what she is doing in actuality is reliving her own youth through me. She likes to buy me pretty items of clothing now and sometimes even surprises me with a purchase she has made for me when taking a shopping trip into Cologne.

My dancing partner is a young high school senior and we dance well together. While he is a good-looking young man, I do not feel any particular attraction towards him. I love to dance, and finally the day arrives for the final ball, given at a rather prestigious Cologne Country Club. After hours of primping in front of the bathroom mirror, driving my father absolutely crazy because everything about my appearance has to be perfect, I take the bus, meet up with my girl friends, and together we make our way by trolley to the big event. The huge ballroom is decked out beautifully with flowers and there is a lovely dinner with intermittent dancing, culminating in the dance competition. This consists of four dances with a team of judges eliminating couples as the dances progress. There is a Waltz, a Quickstep and a Bolero, after which 3 couples are left on the dance floor. My partner and I are among them. The last dance, a Tango, is one of my favorites and we actually win the competition. I am speechless and totally happy as I stand on the stage with my partner, receiving a big bouquet of flowers and a certificate to participate free of charge in the advanced dance course.

The remainder of the evening I am asked to dance by many other young men and I dance until I am exhausted. At one point I go outside on the terrace to catch some fresh air with a young man who asks if I would allow him to drive me home in his father's car. To the great disappointment of my steady dancing partner I accept, since I am rather attracted to this particular young man. When he stops at my house to drop me off, he pulls me towards him and kisses me intensely. I am smitten and we date for a while, until his ex-girl friend returns from a prolonged stay at a Sanatorium for TB in the Alps. It is a shattering experience but we manage to remain good friends anyway.

After taking the advanced ballroom dancing course and also winning that contest with my new and charming dance partner, my social life begins to take shape. Every weekend is spent at the Dancing School. There are dances every Saturday night and every Sunday afternoon. Eventually I become part of the "inner circle" of dance enthusiasts, and while I am still seeing my friends from high school, more and more of my spare time is taken up with the activities at the Dancing School in Cologne. Since I do not allow this to interfere with my grades at school my parents don't object, as a matter of fact, quite often my mother walks with me to the bus station and we talk about fashion trends and dancing. My father, having grown up in the country, never liked dancing. My mother, on the contrary, used to love going out when she was young. As long as I get home at the proper time that is set for me, she is happy that I am having fun.

About this time my sister gets married, and while in the beginning I miss her a lot, my time is taken up with schoolwork, dancing every Saturday night and working Sunday afternoons at her in-laws' bakery, then taking the trolley into Cologne for the Sunday dance parties between the hours of 6 and 8 p.m. This usually gets me home by 9.30 and makes my father happy. Papa is not one to socialize and Mama would have been much happier if he showed some interest going into the city once in a while, strolling along the Rhine or going window shopping, stopping off at a café for some afternoon cake and coffee. But Papa is a country boy at heart and that will never change. They are so very different in taste and temperament that oftentimes I wonder what attracted them to each other in the first place. I vow never to make the same mistake in my life since it is very apparent to me now, as a teenager, that much of their arguments and strife are caused by the fundamental differences in their personalities. While opposites attract, if they are in the realm of my parents' extent, they eventually drive people apart, leading to a rather unfulfilling life. With all the activity I am involved in and now, that my sister is married, having the luxury of my own room, it enables me to distance myself even more from their disagreements, although the tension is sometimes unavoidable and still upsetting to me. Whenever the stress-levels rise due to my home-life or to increased demands at school, the anxiety sets in and I suffer from stomach aches and headaches.

My last year in high school is very difficult and demanding but there are always the weekends to look forward to. My group of friends in Cologne, the ballroom dancers I meet up with, are great people and we date within the group. There is a core of about 20 youngsters and a few of them have cars or are allowed to drive their parents' cars. It is a great relief to me when I am driven home at night, because ever so often I miss the last bus on a Saturday evening after taking the trolley from Cologne into the suburbs. Then I have to walk home. From the bus terminal it is about 4 miles to my home and walking this distance all alone at night is not something I like to do. However, more often than not I can't afford a taxi and so I walk in the middle of the dark streets, which is rather scary at times. All I can hear is the sound of my spiked heels on the dark pavement. I am very grateful each time I arrive home safely and fall into bed. One Saturday evening one of the young students in my dance group whom I have been dating takes me to the trolley stop and is concerned for my safe return home. Since this is the last trolley he cannot accompany me, but to my greatest astonishment he pulls a small handgun out of his pocket and hands it to me. I have never touched a gun in my life and I ask him where he got it. Apparently it is his father's and he offers it to me for protection. Holding the cool handle beautified by mother-of-pearl in my hand, I am very reluctant to take him up on his offer. I will probably shoot myself in the foot, I think, but he assures me that it is safe for me to take, teaching me how to unlock the safety mechanism. Still very reluctant, I put it in the pocket of my coat and promise him to return it the following week. On the entire way home I am terribly worried. I am breaking the law here, me, the most law-abiding citizen in all of Germany! As I walk home that night my hand clutches the cold gun in my coat pocket and I pray that I will not have to use it. My hand is shaking with fear. But I make it home safely. Now of course the problem presents itself what to do with the gun so my parents will not find it. Finally I decide to stash it way underneath my underwear in my dresser where it stays until the following Saturday, when I take it back and hand it over to the young college student, glad to be rid of it. That is the only time I have ever held a gun in my hand and my parents do not find out for another 20 years.

I tell them about my experience one night while they are visiting. They can hardly believe my story because it is so unlike me. Ultimately we all laugh at the fact that there was a gun in the house and other than me nobody knew about it. These are some of the "stupid" things that happen in the lives of even the most sensible and reliable teenagers.

My sister seems to have turned into an "old lady" since she got married. Every time she comes to visit and sees me going out to dance, she complains that I get to enjoy more freedoms than she did, but then again I am the youngest in the family and usually that is the case. I resent her telling my mother to restrict me in my activities because I remember all too well her "activities" when we took that vacation years ago to the Black Forest.

Had my parents known about that, they certainly would not have been happy. I feel that I am entitled to have a social life, considering that my grades in school are very good and that I have a job as well. As a matter of fact, I never ask my mother for money any longer to spend on personal items such as nail polish, lipstick, or hairspray. I disregard what she says and simply chalk it up to her having become married and boring. Plus she seems to have become a total slave to her spouse which annoys me. Why should a woman be subservient to a man? In my mind I will never marry someone who will not accept me as a full partner; never in a million years. She does not even know how much money her husband earns. At home Papa always brings home the money at the end of the month, puts in on the table where he allows me to count it, then gives it to Mama who handles the finances. Although theirs is a troubled marriage, in that respect it functions well and I don't think of my father any less because he lets Mama handle the money.

Not once during this time do I run into a problem, although at times I have anxious moments. I don't understand why this happens.

That year my mother and I return to East Germany for our summer vacation and visit Uncle Otto and Aunt Frieda once more. Again we cross the border at Worlfsburg and, as I notice after entering East Germany, nothing has changed in all the years I last visited. The ominous watchtowers are still there, manned with East German soldiers holding their drawn weapons.

The old women are still working in the fields with hoes and the towns and villages we pass still look neglected and in dire need of repair. Likewise the people from East Germany still look at us suspiciously and with great envy, making me feel extremely uncomfortable. Nobody talks and so my mother and I sit there quietly just looking out of the train window. I have chosen this visit as my project for a lengthy composition required for my high school graduation, but I do not dare take notes. Instead I try to remember as much as I can.

Nothing has changed in the house of my uncle either. Uncle Otto himself though is not the same man I used to know. His hair turned white overnight when he lost his only son. My cousin had studied in East Germany to become an engineer. He was about the age of my oldest sister. Shortly after he graduated he, his fiancee and a friend had taken a ride in his new Wartburg automobile. In a curve he had lost control of his car and hit a tree. The steering wheel crushed his chest and he died instantly. After that Uncle Otto fell into a deep depression from which he never recovered. Even the fact that his daughter had gotten married and is carrying his first grandchild seems of little consolation to him. He is kind towards me as is my aunt, but my mother leaves after a week and I spend the next two weeks keenly observing how East Germany is functioning or rather not functioning very well. By then Uncle Otto has stopped attending the weekly political meetings. He just does not care any longer. He complains bitterly that there is a shortage of everything, from roofing nails to toilets or bathtubs, items readily available in West Germany. However, he still does not dare to turn his television antenna in the direction of West Germany in order to receive West German programs, because it is too dangerous. You never know if one of your neighbors is a member of the Stasi, the much dreaded "secret police" which is spying on people.

It all makes for a stifling atmosphere and I do not envy them. That summer it is hot but there is no public swimming pool, just an old quarry filled with water and no longer in use. At one point it is very deep, and through the crystal clear water I can see all the way to the bottom. That is where I go on hot days with my very pregnant cousin to cool off. It is very refreshing and sometimes her husband, a Russian and physical education teacher by profession, accompanies us. He is a staunch Communist. We have many heated discussions and open disagreements. Since he has never had the opportunity to visit West Germany, by now totally recovered from the war, I do not think he has the right or the knowledge to make any judgements and I tell him so. There are times he becomes very defensive and hostile. Actually I really do not care for him very much. He is so very narrow-minded.

In a certain way though I enjoy the simple country life, taking long walks in the woods, visiting my grandparents' and cousin's gravesites, the Schrebergarten they still rent, just sitting and admiring the ancient red beech nearby planted by Napoleon's troops. But in general I find life in East Germany extraordinarily boring. Once a week I am again required to present myself to the Communist Authorities and I am pressed for my opinion, trying my very best to circumvent tricky questions designed to confuse me or give an answer that would have displeased them. One day Tante Frieda and I take a ride by train to the village in the Harz Mountains where my cousin lives. Even the trains have not changed at all. They are the very same steam locomotives with their ancient, hard wooden seats and they are dirty. Everything seems to be covered with grime, the waiting rooms, the public toilets, and the grocery stores.

It gives the impression that time has stood still here and that the people have just given up. Religion is outlawed. The churches are closed and what used to be Confirmation or First Communion has now been replaced by what the Communist government calls "Jugendweihe," a ritual arranged by the Party formally introducing the youngsters to the junior ranks of the Communist regime.

Coming from West Germany and having had the opportunity to travel abroad, I am sincerely happy when the three weeks of my stay are up. I have enough material for my composition and bidding my Uncle Otto good-bye at the train station, I see tears rolling down his cheeks. He is a sad and broken man.

Returning to West Germany proves to be quite an adventure, since the train is held up on the East German side of the border for hours. The young soldiers of the border patrol are extremely rude and one of them, after questioning me where I had stayed, actually has me open my suitcase and then simply dumps the entire contents on the dirty floor of the train. I am furious but have to keep quiet. Once the train is finally allowed to leave, I am joined in my compartment by a young woman with a little two-year-old boy. The young woman's eyes are almost completely swollen shut from crying. Visiting her parents in East Germany she had been given by her father a stamp-collection for her son. When finding it amongst her possessions, the East German guards took her off the train the previous evening, then detained and interrogated her all through the night. They threatened her with the accusation of misappropriating State Property. After 12 hours she was finally allowed to leave, however without the stamp-collection her father had given her.

The ordeal has shaken her to the core, and during the train ride back she begins to cry again on several occasions. I take the little boy on my lap, tell him stories and play games with him in order to allow the mother to regain her bearings.

In my report about the conditions in East Germany I hold nothing back, not the rotten infrastructure, the general lack of consumer items, the terrible condition of towns and villages, the repression of the people, and how the younger generation by now has been totally brainwashed by the Communist Party. The report earns me an A for my final in

German composition. I vow never to return, because it has been a depressing experience and I feel sorry for the people who have just given up and accepted their fate, all the while deeply resenting West Germans.

We are within the last six months prior to graduating from high school when I am approached by my Math teacher asking me to help some of my class-mates who are having trouble making the grade. He suggests I act as a tutor for them and gets in touch with their parents, asking them to pay me for my efforts. So we meet twice a week at my house and I am delighted that I am not only doing my homework while at the same time explaining the problems to my class-mates, which in turn makes them clearer to me, but that I earn money in the bargain. My teacher suggests that I might wish to pursue a career in teaching: however, I have no particular interest in this field and am looking for something more exciting. To everybody's satisfaction I am able to pull my friends up to passing grades, some even up to the equivalent of an American B-.

Suddenly all kinds of money-making possibilities open up to me. Some of my girl friends like the way I style my hair and are unable to fix their own. They come to my house on a Saturday prior to a date and I fix it for them. Even though I would gladly do it as an act of friendship, they insist on paying me, for otherwise they would have had to go to a Beauty Parlor. I save my money diligently and it pays for a pair of dancing shoes, the type used by professional ballroom dancers. Suddenly it seems as though everything is falling into place and happening at once. The shy little girl I once was is beginning to spread her wings and to act on the steps it will take to turn into the Tumbleweed of her dreams.

At the Dancing School the owner approaches eight of our group, including me, with the idea of forming a group of good dancers to perform on special occasions in costumes of the Flapper era. He is willing to have costumes specially tailored for us and pay for them. The plan is, that we will perform for the School free of charge during the final balls given at the Country Club for each group of new students, our photos will be in the printed brochure for advertising purposes and we will be able to partake in the school dance activities and special dances free of charge from now on. Naturally we accept and are very excited about the prospects of going on stage. In addition to the above, we are allowed to perform for a fee, if asked to provide entertainment for corporate Christmas Parties and similar functions. We may use the costumes and are allowed to set our own fee.

During the following two months we meet twice a week. We practice two dances which were popular during the Flapper era and have been choreographed for us by the owner of the Dancing School. We have a lot of fun practicing in front of a mirrored wall in one of the smaller rooms of the School. Meanwhile the material for the costumes has been picked out. The ones for the young men will consist of black three-piece suits, spats, hats and a cane in period style, while the costumes for the young ladies are designed in shimmering silver with black fringes, long gloves and a headband to match. An excellent seamstress tailors the costumes for each of us. We have several fittings and finally the day arrives for our first performance.

Eight nervous youngsters are announced via the loudspeaker: "and now, as the highlight of the evening, our special Dance Troupe will be performing for your enjoyment the Tango and the Cha-cha-cha." With clammy hands and pounding hearts we run out from behind the huge curtain in pairs to the introductory music of the orchestra. Everything goes off as planned and all of us bow gracefully to the applause. What a feeling! The first few times we relish the "celebrity status" after the performance, but eventually it turns into a routine the way everything does, if it is done often enough. During the holiday season that year requests come in for performances at Christmas Parties given by corporations for their employees. We gladly accept. Not only do we have a lot of fun, but the pay is good and, as a bonus, we get to participate in the lavish festivities, always given in the finest locations of Cologne and offering gourmet food and drink. The laws in Germany concerning under-age drinking are quite lax, but none of us ever abuses the privilege. We usually have a couple of glasses of wine or champagne with our dinner, then switch to soft drinks for the rest of the evening.

By now I rarely socialize any longer with my friends from school since my entire focus has shifted to the activities in Cologne proper and the exposure to this new world is gradually reflected in my feeling more self-assured. It often baffles me that I am totally comfortable going on stage performing without any sign of anxiety whatsoever, but that on other occasions, when nothing in particular is bothering me, the feeling of utter panic totally engulfs me. I simply do not understand what is causing me to feel this way.

The spring of my high school graduation I am hit with some disturbing news. After having consulted a physician regarding my occasional feelings of dizziness and panic involving a complete physical, I am told that I am suffering from curvature of the spine and it is recommended that I wear a plaster corset for a year. Devastated, I cry for days.

Just when things were looking up, just when I was beginning to feel a measure of freedom and self-esteem, I am confronted with this health problem that can change my life for years to come. Once I regain my composure I return to the physician with Mama, who at this time is delighted with my social life.

We talk to the physician about a possible alternative. After all, wearing a plaster corset would mean I would have to give up dancing. Other than my school work nothing is more important to me now, since it provides me with a good social outlet and also fulfills my passion for combining music with movement. I am given the alternative of having a professional back-massage three times a week at a local spa and swim once a week, breast-stroke, for at least one hour. This will strengthen my back muscles and prevent any further curvature that would necessitate a more radical approach. I gladly settle for that, and for the next year and a half I keep my appointments with the professional masseur and I am a regular every Saturday at the local in-door swimming pool. Knowing what is at stake I swim for a solid hour pacing myself and praying the treatment works. This is a small price to pay. I like swimming laps and gradually become less self-conscious about the masseur, a man in his early thirties, who skillfully massages my back three times a week.

My graduation from high school is a memorable occasion. Even though I qualify for both, the prize for best achievements in languages and science, being a girl I receive the prize for languages. The photo of the principle handing out the prizes can be seen in the local newspapers.

My parents are very proud of me and the photo from the local paper will hang in their kitchen for years to come. The final tests were difficult and we are glad to have passed this period of our lives, celebrating that night with a big Graduation Party. Again the press is there and photos are taken in particular of the winners of the book prizes, this time in our evening wear. That night most teachers we have had over the years attend. Our much loved French teacher, adored by all the female students, who had transferred to a different school a year ago, shows up as a surprise. It turns out to be even more of a memorable evening than I could have expected. He asks me to dance frequently and offers to drive me home at the end of the graduation festivities. My girl friend Ute is staying overnight at my house. When we get there my former French teacher actually gives both of us a kiss. To my greatest surprise I receive a long French kiss. I am bewildered and happy at the same time. This is an enormously charming married man in his late thirties, whom we all have adored from afar. Ute and I talk about it at length prior to falling asleep. After about a week I do not give the matter any further thought. He must have been slightly tipsy, I think.

However, during the following week I receive in the mail a postcard from him in French, asking me to meet him at a Cologne restaurant on a certain day at a certain hour. He will be waiting there for me. The message ends with "grose bise" (big kiss) and I consult my girl-friends from high school the next day. Should I go or not? I am positively terrified! The overriding consensus is that I am a fool if I don't go, after all, just go and see what he wants, I am told. That afternoon I don't tell my parents where I am going, simply that I have to take care of something in Cologne. I walk into the restaurant where he is waiting at the appointed hour with shaky knees. We talk at length about my plans for the future, he is extremely charming and I try my best to act as adult as possible. After dinner he offers to take me home. On the way there the road leads through a park near my house where he suddenly pulls over, stops and begins to make unexpected advances.

"How naïve of me," I think, "I should have seen this coming." He notices my reluctance but nevertheless asks if it is possible for me to get away from home for a week. Spring vacation is here and he can make a reservation for us at a certain monastery no less, where he goes for a retreat once in a while.

According to his description the friars are pretty worldly and this is yet another incident, which makes me question my Catholic upbringing. The friars know this man is married and I am sure I am not the first young lady he takes there on a "retreat." I tell him that I don't think I want to go there, at which point he becomes angry, accusing me of having led him on and pulls me towards him forcefully. A struggle ensues. I actually scratch his face, fighting to get out of the car and walk the rest of the way home in tears. In retrospect this really was a bad idea. I see him once more on the occasion of a farewell party given by our class-room teacher who, judging by their familiarity, most likely was one of his lovers in the past. Once more he tries to corner me on the balcony of my teacher's apartment, but I resist and that is the last time I see him. In the future, I decide, it is not a wise choice to place too much trust into a teacher, a lesson that will serve me well.

The College Years

During my last year in high school I go through the typical agony, making a decision as to what to do with the rest of my life. Since I am equally talented in the sciences as in the language department, this is a rough decision for me. Ultimately I decide on languages, since there is the possibility of extensive travel in this field. At the time the three best schools for language students striving to become translators or interpreters in Germany are Heidelberg, Germersheim and Cologne. I don't receive any encouragement from my parents and it is not a financial matter, since the education is free. I am more than willing to pay for the books myself.

Mama thinks I should simply become a secretary at a local company since I will get married in the future anyhow. Basically my parents consider my efforts a waste. But I am determined to further my education, and go ahead with the application for the entrance examination at the Dolmetscherschule der Stadt Koeln which is affiliated with the University of Cologne, but housed in a different area. Nowadays there is no entrance examination requirement and I found out during a visit from my favorite former professor in the late 80's, that subsequently the performance standards dropped dramatically. "They don't make them like you any more," he said at the time, and I was pleased to realize he knew how hard I worked to achieve my goal. I apply with 2 other students from my high school class. On the morning of the entrance examination we set out together on the lengthy commute. In order to get there I have to get up at 4.30 a.m., take a bus and three trolleys to be there at 7.30 a.m. The auditorium is filled with nervous applicants.

Looking around, I find many of the applicants to be considerably older than I am. While I am 17, some are in their 30's and have spent a year or longer in the United States, Canada or Great Britain as au pairs. That recognition is intimidating to say the least. We are divided into language majors. I have applied to major in English and minor in French. When the examination starts you can hear a pin drop. At first we take the English tests, consisting of a dictation, a composition and a general test of skills. It is extremely difficult and I am wondering what I am doing here. Then, during the French exam, I just want to give up and go home. What was I thinking? I don't even understand half of the dictation and my anxiety levels reach new heights. I almost have to excuse myself because I feel I cannot breathe.

On the way home we discuss the difficulty of the examinations and none of us feel we have any chance of passing. The test results will be send out by mail in about a month. I know I definitely failed French, but something tells me that my English might be o.k. Nevertheless, three rather dejected high-school students arrive back home in the suburbs. The next four weeks seem like the longest weeks of my life. Then, one day, I arrive at home and there is an official looking letter next to my dinner plate. Mama is looking at me with curious "well open it" eyes! I am scared, for I feel I am holding my future in my hands and in reality I do. Finally I cannot stand the suspense any longer and open the letter, unfold it and there it states, briefly and to the point, that I passed the English exam but failed in French. However they are willing to accept me because of my strong showing in English. I read the letter about a dozen times and dance around the kitchen with joy. Yes, I realize this is going to be hard, but here is my path to freedom. I will succeed! I will do anything, work any amount of hours, have no social life at all, do whatever it takes but I will become an interpreter and translator. That will open the world to me.

Even though my parents are still not supportive, I detect they are proud of me because my father takes it upon himself to ride his bicycle to the local newspaper and the next issue carries an article: "Fraeulein Inge Bose, recently graduated with Honors from High School and has been accepted as a student at the Dolmetscherschule der Stadt Koeln. She plans to major in English and travel abroad. So he is proud of me after all, even though in later years he will say many times to me:

"The worst decision I ever made was sending you to College!" And I used to think but not say: "You did not send me to College, I did that all by myself."

He likewise blamed my dating habits, always dating young men from foreign countries, as well as the fact that I left Germany for the United States, on my education. Little did he realize that it was my salvation!

Since learning has always been fun for me, I very much look forward to the first day although I am quite intimidated. None of the other fellow students of my high school who took the entrance exam passed, meaning that I don't know a soul and have to make new friends. The first semester starts on April lst. and classes are Monday through Friday. Even though I will have a very long commute, I will be off on Saturdays and thus be able to have a little social life after all. Plus there will be a month off in March and a semester break of two months during August and September. Consequently I can work for some time, save and travel during the remainder of the vacation.

And so my rigorous studies as well as the endless commute begin. A 17 year old girl is not exactly overjoyed having to get up at 4.30 a.m. every morning, walk to a bus station in all kinds of weather, take the bus and then change twice, arriving by trolley car just in time for the first class. But then I get used to everything unpleasant rather easily by now, having acquired the attitude that whatever it takes, it can be done! The first day does not start out too well for me. Somehow I was given the Attendance Book and since the Interpreter's College shares the building with some of the Economics Department of Cologne University, the mostly male students are having a good look at the freshmen students of my class, mostly female. By now I am no longer the "ugly duckling" and a number of economics students involve me in a conversation. I miss seeing the professor enter and the rest of the class going into the auditorium. A couple of minutes later the professor sticks his head out of the door and asks me in a rather sarcastic fashion if I care to join them, in particular since I am in charge of the Attendance Book. Turning red like a beet I enter quickly and thus on the first day everyone knows who I am! No, I did not make a good first impression and it was really not my intention to come across as the "flighty" type of student.

The first few days are very difficult, so much so that I am seriously thinking of throwing in the towel, giving up and doing something else. Most students in my English classes have been abroad and are older. There are only three of us who are the same age and at about the same level: Susanne, Eva and me. Naturally we feel drawn together and become friends, sharing the breaks in between classes and sitting together during lectures. There is no way I can catch up to the level required in French and so I decide to switch over to Spanish, a beginner's course, which Susanne and Eva chose right from the outset. I really don't like Spanish very much but it is the only alternative open to me and I take this new path. As long as I can get my degree in English, that is all I care about. Starting Spanish from the beginning I am allowed to drop it after two semesters. Having made the decision to work as hard as I can, I throw myself with all I have into my studies, which means leaving my house every morning at 5a.m., getting home by 2.30 p.m., eating, napping for one hour and then resuming my studies only to be interrupted by dinner. At 9 p.m. I fall into bed totally exhausted. Also I make it a point to become a member of the two English libraries in Cologne, "Die Bruecke" (which offers all the British classics) and "Das Amerika Haus" (with all the American classics). They happen to be located where I have to switch trolleys and so instead of wasting time waiting for the next trolley, I go and pick out books. For the next seven semesters I will read two English books a week, which eventually leads to my having read most of the British and American classic literature, but also to the command of a better and wider range of vocabulary than the average student. My natural love for books and reading comes in very handy at this point, and I begin to actually enjoy my lengthy commute. It beats staring out of the window and seeing the same scenery day after day, although I always take my eyes off the pages when the trolley crosses the Rhine river. Even on a dreary day, and Cologne has many, the view of the wide river and the imposing Gothic Cathedral with its tall spires is a beautiful sight.

Susanne, Eva and I become good friends and get to know just about everything regarding our home lives. Susanne's mother is divorced with 5 daughters; things are not easy financially. Like me, Eva was born out of wedlock but adopted by her mother's husband and she has a younger sister.

None of us have had an easy childhood. While Susanne and I are blue-eyed and have long blond hair, Eva has dark brown eyes and black shoulder-length hair. None of us have a steady boyfriend at this time, but we are beginning to turn heads amongst the male student body.

During the first semester it becomes very clear to me that my weakest point is conversational English, and I decide that it is necessary for me to spend some time in Great Britain by myself, thus being forced to rely only on my own knowledge of the English language. The previous Carnival season I made the acquaintance of a young British policeman whom I have been corresponding with. He arranges for me to get a room with the same landlady where he lives in Yorkshire. I have some money saved up and make reservations for my trip. My parents don't object, which in retrospect surprises me, all the more since I will be gone for a month by myself. I just turned 18 and there is a mail-strike going on in England. As yet we do not own a telephone. But then by now I have shed my timidity and gained a sense of purpose, a drive to succeed at any cost. The situation at home is the same. There are heated battles mainly on weekends between my parents and often I don't even feel like getting out of bed. Yet somehow I manage to get through it all. I do at this time show a lot of physical symptoms though caused by anxiety and feeling laden with guilt, guilt for having been born, being German with a despicable past which no teacher, professor or foreigner allows me to forget. I continue to have dizzy spells and vicious migraine headaches, apparently inherited from my mother who at least once a month comes down with a horrific migraine herself. I feel sorry for her because I know how debilitating this can be. Like her, sometimes it takes days of lying quietly in a darkened room vomiting until there is nothing left in my stomach. During one of these attacks I faint in the bathroom and my father has to carry me upstairs to my bed.

Strangely enough Susanne and Eva likewise show physical symptoms much like mine, another thing we have in common and which forges an ever closer bond between us. We understand when one of us feels ill after undergoing a stressful time in our homes, not even considering the stress of being the youngest students at this time attending our College.

The night prior to my first trip to England I spend with friends at our Dancing School, as a matter of fact, I sleep over at a friend's house. After a totally sleepless night due to the excitement of the trip, I leave with my suitcase early in the morning to board the train for Oostend, Belgium, in order to catch the ferry there which will take me across the English Channel to Dover. Since we miss one ferry due to a delay in the train ride, I attach myself to a group of young students and get to spend a night with a very nice host couple in a lovely suburb of London. Their daughter is kind enough to drive me into town the following day for me to catch the train from Victoria Station to my final destination in Yorkshire. Because I am a day late now the landlady, a lovely elderly widow named Mrs. White, ("Whitey" for short as she likes to be called) is surprised but has my room ready. Being a widow with a small pension she supplements her income by renting out rooms and cooking for her boarders. I will pay her for room and board for three weeks, then travel to London for the last week. Being there by myself my English improves quickly and I have a very nice time. Friends of Whitey's take me to the town of York with its lovely University, I get to cross the Humber and spend a day of sightseeing in the port city of Hull. There is even a shopping spree to the town of Leeds. These are the beginning stages of the "Mods" and "Rockers," the Beatles have just launched the movie "HELP", in short, England is THE swinging place to be. Comments are being made about "the BLOODY GERMANS," but being a pretty 18 year old girl anxious to absorb the British culture, I am "forgiven" for my wretched ancestry. Thus my experience in general is positive.

Whitey and I become rather fond of one another. She is the grandmotherly type and quite outspoken which I like. When I leave for London tears are shed on both sides.

Once back at Victoria Station I hire the traditional black cab inclusive Cockney cabdriver and ask him to drop me off at a nice WYCA anywhere, preferably somewhere in the very heart of London. I end up in a Youth Hostel in Marylebone, right smack in the center of all the activity and a nice safe area from which to explore the city. During the train journey I compiled a list of "MUST SEE" attractions and historic sites to visit, buy a map and the next morning I am on my way. Looking back I still marvel at the ease with which I explore this large metropolitan city and how I conquer it almost entirely on foot. A few times I take a bus, intrigued by the Double-Decker phenomenon and astounded by the civility of the British people, the way they queue up patiently. "If this were Germany," I think, "people would be using their elbows pushing and shoving to get onto the bus first." I like the civility. It is like a breath of fresh air. After visiting the Houses of Parliament, Westminster Abbey, Trafalgar Square, Piccadilly Circle, Speaker's Corner, Buckingham Palace where I watch the Changing of the

Guard and Madame Toussaud's, an American College student, who is two years older than me, asks if she can join me. Together we visit the British Museum, the Tower of London in its entirety plus Tower Bridge, St. Paul's Cathedral as well as Fleet Street, center of the British press. The week goes by in a flash. My feet are sore but I feel I have accomplished what I set out to do. I have not spoken one German word in a little over a month. A young French student who also stays with a group at the youth hostel asks me to go to the movies with him. He is cute and I accept. We go to see the Beatles in "HELP." Even then I find the music great but the movie rather mediocre, however I miss a lot anyway since the young Frenchman is rather charming and an excellent kisser, a trait much appreciated by any young girl.

Sadly the day arrives for me to leave and I return by train to Dover, catch the ferry back to Oostend where during the crossing of the English Channel I am treated to observing a young group of Scottish lads performing the ancient sword-dance on the upper deck.

Boarding the train back to Cologne my mood turns dark and the closer I get to my hometown, the more depressed I get. Back at the train station of the suburb where I live, I call a taxi and the driver asks me where I come from. "LONDON," I proudly proclaim, and he marvels at a girl my age travelling to England all by herself. He drops me off at home where I find out that my mother has been sent to a Spa for six weeks. She has not been feeling well and her nerves in particular are giving her problems. So it is just Papa and me. These days we do not get along too well, the typical scenario of my immature behavior feeling very "wordly" and his resentment about working two jobs. He still does wall-paper hanging and house painting aside from

141

his full-time position at the railroad, as well as taking care of the big yard including a huge vegetable garden. Vegetable gardens have not yet given way to the lawn-craze American style. The memory of going hungry is not easily forgotten. After about a week of bickering and unpleasantness I take the train to pay Mama a visit at the Spa and complain bitterly about Papa's bad moods. In a sick way he is very dependent on her for everything.

Even though she verbally abuses him constantly, when she is not around he misses her terribly and is miserable company. He loves her so much it hurts and oftentimes I feel sorry for him. But then again, he too has his own ways of driving a person mad; the two of them are just like oil and water. I wonder at this age whether it was just the physical attraction which drew my father to my mother and her desperate need to find another provider? I shall never know. While visiting Mama she suggests I take another trip, since I don't have to return to College until October 1st. The previous year the couple my parents have stayed with at their hotel on the Italian Riviera came to visit us and there is an open invitation to reciprocate. She suggests I go and visit them. So on a whim I pack my suitcase once more. I think Papa is actually glad I am leaving, and since we do not have a telephone yet I arrive totally unannounced at the Pensione Bella Vista after an 18 hour train ride, which yet again takes me through my beloved Alps. I can ride for free, getting a certain amount of free passes due to Papa's employment with the German Railroad, and even though the Pensione is full, they put up a cot for me in the office and I am more than welcome.

Bella Vista is located about one half hour walking distance from the beach half-way up a mountain. I have to walk a serpentine road down the mountain with gorgeous views over the Mediterranean but I don't mind the walk at all which takes me through fig and olive groves. Now in September they are ripening and the fragrances are sweet and foreign.

Many times on my way back from the beach I stop and sit on a rock outcropping, just drinking in the wonder all around me: the beautiful sunshine, weather every German longs for, with pleasant temperatures, blue skies and flowers in the most vivid colors. I can just sit, daydream for hours and feel totally at peace.

Being 18 and having long blond hair is a big plus in Italy, so I don't lack potential suitors. But they are rather forward and I am cautious with the acquaintances I make. While sitting on a bench by the beach a young man named Roberto notices one day that I am reading an English book, and he proudly proclaims that he too has been to England. We date a few times until his advances become too bold and I decide, that in spite of his being strikingly handsome, I am not ready for what he has in mind. One word I never have trouble with saying is "NO" and meaning it, which is a good thing and will always serve me well.

The "Papagallo" phenomenon, young Italian men seducing young Nordic girls is in full swing and German tabloids are full of stories dealing with young girls who return home from an Italian vacation with "excess" luggage. At this time that is the furthest thing on my mind. I want to have a career, travel the world, get out of my miserable household and be free to soar like an eagle. I even have dreams now and then of being able to fly. I dream I can take off by just flapping my arms, fly anywhere and it feels absolutely wonderful.

After three weeks on the Italian Riviera I return to Cologne suntanned and happy. As chance would have it, I end up with the same taxi driver I hired when returning from England. He looks at me with questioning eyes through the rear-view mirror and says: "Young Lady, did I not drive you home just a few weeks ago?" "Yes," I answer feeling very worldly. But then I was returning from London, this time I am returning from Genoa." He shakes his head and I hear him making a comment to the effect, "that some people have all the luck." Little does he know how hard I worked for my trips, saved every penny, made my own clothes and took any job available to me in order to have travel money. Naturally the free railroad tickets through my father's employment come in handy, for otherwise I most likely would not be able to afford that much travel.

Meanwhile Mama has returned from the Spa and Papa is in a better frame of mind. I return to the University a little more sure of myself and indeed, the effort of spending a month in Great Britain not speaking any German at all has paid off. My conversational English has improved tremendously and I no longer hesitate to partake in the discussion groups. Naturally I speak with a British accent, while some of my fellow-students have an American or Canadian accent. However, as we are in Europe, the British English is preferred and we say "lorry" instead of "truck," "motorway" instead of "highway." Students are encouraged to use pure English and I am making great strides. Susanne, Eva and I are still the best of friends and get together frequently, either to study or socialize, though most of my own social life still revolves around ballroom dancing and the Dance Troupe I am a member of. The owner of the Dancing School allows us to use the costumes to get engagements for special events in Cologne, and this provides further money for my travel fund. By now we have become quite good at performing our routine.

Then there is the student hangout, the Café Paris, which only allows students and strictly checks our student identification cards. It becomes our favorite place on Saturday nights. Smokey with loud music of the 60s, it is filled to the brim with students from all over the world and an interesting place to meet young men. There is no excessive drinking. Actually most students simply don't have the money and nurture a beer or a coke all night.

Unfortunately it is located in the center of Cologne, so Susanne, Eva and I have to leave earlier than most to catch the last trolley home. All of us live far away in the suburbs and hardly any of the students have the luxury of owning a car.

I work very hard during the winter months and after the second semester pass the State Examination, which entitles me to call myself a Foreign Language Correspondent. Some of the students leave after attaining this goal, but to me the work they will perform seems like that of a glorified secretary. I want to continue my education plus I can now drop Spanish which I never truly enjoyed in the first place. Nevertheless I pass my examination with a satisfactory grade.

That spring my parents ask me what I would like to have for my birthday.

I do not wait an instant and answer: "I want my "Dracula teeth" fixed. So for my birthday I have one front eye tooth pulled, another tooth ground down and a crown made which looks better than what I had, yet my front teeth are still rather crooked. A painful birthday gift but much appreciated, I guess these days it would be comparable to a young girl asking for a "nose job" as a gift. Anyway, I am

145

smiling more often these days and don't feel quite so self-conscious about my appearance any longer.

Continuing my Education

The number of students in my class has shrunken considerably. The "dead-wood," the girls with wealthy parents whose daughters did not make the grade is gone, as are those who chose to become a Foreign Correspondent.

What are left are the serious students who wish to continue. Classes consist of no more than 20 students at this time. The requirements move up a notch, and I decide to take three semesters in order to achieve a better grade on my Translator's Certificate. It is well worth the extra semester. By now I am really starting to have fun and have a wide circle of friends, even though Susanne, Eva and I are still the closest. I try to distance myself as much as I can from my dysfunctional home life by sequestering myself as often as I can and for as long as I can in my room, along with my little portable radio. It has been handed down to me by my sister. I listen to the "British Invasion," as a matter of fact the radio goes wherever I go. My mother must have reached the pre-menopausal phase about now and her moods are ever more erratic. Papa is experiencing a lot of stress at work which does not help the situation. Poor Tante Grete, who has been living in the former shack which was fixed up for her since my last years in high school seems to catch the brunt of it all.

For whatever reason, all of a sudden she has become "the main enemy" in my mother's life. I feel very badly for the verbal abuse she is subjected to.

Mama has also become rather anti-social and reclusive. Other than doing her daily shopping, she rarely goes out these days and I think that is part of her problem. It leaves her too much time to spend thinking about past and present resentments. Her anxieties and depression are not something one talks about in Germany. It seems the country that brought forth Freud, (actually he like Hitler were Austrian) is light-years removed from modern mental health care and so the signs go undetected.

The aftereffects of WWII, the post-traumatic stress remains untreated. I think I would have had more empathy for Mama, had I known what she was going through. Since I don't her frequent remarks "my nerves just cannot take it any longer," can make me very angry. "My own nerves are not in good shape either," I think to myself, "and you are the reason for it."

How can I know at this age that there are millions of people in Germany, civilians like my mother and father, who are going through the same emotions and since they are not allowed to voice them, will end up carrying them to their graves. Suicide is a very popular option in that demographic age group it seems, but I fail to make the connection.

Although at this time my own condition is less reflected by anxiety, it expresses itself in physical symptoms, such as stomach aches and vicious migraines, something Susanne and Eva also suffer from. Deep down I know there is something wrong with me. Oftentimes I or my friends have to excuse ourselves from classes and go home since we don't feel well.

The Vietnam War is in full swing and the papers record daily how many Americans were killed the day before. Nobody in Europe stands behind this crazy war and it is the topic of many discussions during classes as well as afterwards, when as a group we mill about waiting for our trolleys to take us home in different directions. It is hotly debated what the purpose of the American involvement is and anti-American sentiments run high. Being young students of course, we are at times rather irreverent about the entire matter. A new male student who transferred from the University of Germersheim regularly refers to the way I part my hair in the middle as the "Ho-Chi Min Trail." I come to accept his teasing. He is a nice, good-looking young man of 28 and an excellent student. Someone like him will end up in the Bundestag or at the UN, much coveted interpreter positions mostly reserved for men, unless one has connections. Even at the University it becomes clear to me, that the old German class system is very much alive.

The fact that someone's father is a professional or owns a business automatically puts them into a higher class than someone like myself, whose father is employed by the railroad. There is no escaping it. Your background more or less dictates how far and where you will go. It is a constant thorn in my side, because by now I very much have come to stand on my own two feet and wish to take responsibility for my own fate. Yet, I feel painfully restricted due to my upbringing and who my parents are.

True, nobody knows any longer that I was born out of wedlock or of my humble beginnings, and also these are the 60's, the years of the "German Economic Miracle."

There is a general mood of optimism in the country. However, the class system is something deeply ingrained and hard to escape from. Once working class it seems, no matter what you achieve on your own, certain avenues and connections are not available to you, no matter how hard you try. Somehow it reminds me of the Indian Caste System.

I continue to enjoy my studies very much. The books I keep reading faithfully open my mind and the University atmosphere fosters the broadening of thought in general.

I totally immerse myself in the experience, grateful that I am able to participate.

Now we also enjoy a certain amount of freedom. We are allowed to miss up to 20% of the semester and still sign up for the final examination, something we occasionally take advantage of. There are times during the winter semester when there are delays by the trolleys, and just by chance we end up meeting at a centrally located point in Cologne. There we decide it is simply too cold and nasty a day for studies. We would be better off and it would be infinitely more beneficial for our little group to retreat to the nearest Café, hang out but speak only English. We learn something, yet we have a lot of fun at the same time. Even though a University education is free other than the purchase of books, students are in a class by themselves, making me realize only much later that I too am guilty of participating in the system of class distinction. In those days I tend to think less of others my age who have chosen to learn a trade. It will take many years of maturing to bring me to this recognition and being in the "trenches" myself, until I will fully realize that no matter what a person does, it is valuable. After all, what would we do without steelworkers, masons, plumbers and electricians? But the folly of youth is just that; the folly of not knowing enough about life. Had I known what I know now, I would not have been ashamed while waiting at the bus station, seeing my father pass by on his way to or back from work riding his old rusty bicycle. He would always wave to me enthusiastically and cheerfully call out my name, while I wanted to become temporarily invisible. Decades later I told him that I was so proud of him, I could not have been any prouder had he been driving a Mercedes Benz. I know it could not take away the pain he must have felt at my reaction, but by then he was understanding and well pleased that I asked his forgiveness for my teenage ignorance. He delighted in the thought that I was proud of him and his own accomplishments.

During the winter of my semesters to become a certified translator I have the opportunity to work for a week at the International Fair for Kitchens and Baths in Cologne, the big "Messe." It pays extremely well and so Eva as well as myself go to apply for a position. We are interviewed separately by a man who is in charge of hiring the required personnel for the "MESSE" and we dress up in our finest. Miniskirts have just come into fashion and I even own a MARY QUANT DRESS. He picks me but not Eva. I feel badly for her. She is a pretty girl but apparently long blond hair is more in demand. I am assigned to a well known German company which produces kitchen appliances with the name that our own kitchen appliances at home bear.

Having worked ahead, I can afford to take the week off and excitedly show up the first day ready to use my English skills, only to find out that in reality I am nothing but a glorified hostess. A pretty face to serve drinks to the sales representatives and their customers. I am not allowed to sit down all day, and by the time I get home that night my feet are swollen. They are so sore I can hardly walk. High heeled shoes are required and so I soak my feet in an herbal footbath, then drop dead-tired into bed wondering how I am going to survive the rest of the week. Some of the company CEO's are rather forward and obnoxious, but I avoid getting caught alone in a sale's cubicle with them and know within a very short time whom to look out for. I make it through the rest of the days wondering if my feet will ever recover from the ordeal, but I have saved up enough money for my next trip abroad, since the tips were excellent. Also the owner of the company has taken a liking to me and even has his chauffeur take me home on the last day in his black Mercedes limousine. Plus he presents me with an expensive gift, a solid gold antique coin over one hundred years old. He also promises that I will be called the following year for the same job when the Trade Fair returns to Cologne and, that, once I graduate from college, he will gladly use his influence in helping me find a good position. Two weeks later I receive a package in the mail with a letter from him and a book, a LOVE STORY! It is then that I realize his intentions are not necessarily the best.

Meanwhile it is almost time for the spring semester break during the month of March, during which Eva and I have made plans to go to England together and stay with Mrs. White in Yorkshire for a month. Eva has never been to England and it will be fun to travel with a friend. She too has saved her money from odd jobs and we should get by. Unfortunately Mrs. White has fallen ill and refers us to another family which, for a certain amount, will house and feed us in their home for three weeks. The woman is an expatriated German who married an Englishman shortly after the war, has two teenage sons and looks forward to having female German company.

Immediately after the semester ends we embark on our journey, take the train again to Oostend in Belgium and the ferry to the White Cliffs of Dover.

The English Channel is well known for rough seas, but the last time I crossed it was in the midst of summer with calm waters. This time the Channel is true to it's reputation and I feel terribly seasick. As a matter of fact, even though it is freezing cold and nasty outside, I prefer to stay on the upper deck and fix my eyes on the horizon in order not to vomit. The passage finally ends and I am never so glad to get off a moving object. We take the train the same day from Victoria Station up to Yorkshire and arrive at our destination by that evening.

The stay with the English/German couple is delightful. Even though it is rather chilly and nasty outside and, like most British homes at the time, central heating is not yet the norm, something that takes getting used to. We curl up in front of the coal burning fireplaces with our teenage "brothers" at night watching TV. All three channels and I don't have to explain to those who are familiar with Britisch Television, that there are a multitude of programs dealing with agriculture and gardening, not exactly teenage TV fare. Having a fireplace as the main heat source is new to us. While we find that our backs are freezing, our fronts are too warm, so much so that one night smoke can be seen curling from the tips of my slippers. I have been trying to warm my feet and accidentally set my slippers on fire. During the daytime we are left to our own devices and explore the town, among others an old English Manor which is now a museum.

We even get a tour of the steel mill where the husband of our host family works.

Both Eva and I find this extremely interesting. The husband is very fond of Eva, in a way, which makes her feel uncomfortable. After a particular incident in the kitchen where he tried to kiss her, she asks me not to leave her alone with him anymore.

Somehow the host wife is totally unaware of her spouse's behavior, as a matter of fact, after we leave once our three weeks are up, she becomes pregnant, gives birth to a baby girl and they name her Eva. I wonder why the wife did not notice what was so very obvious to us?

As a German, married to an English soldier at the end of the war, she did not have an easy life at first. One night, when her husband is on night shift, she tells us her story and I see that here too is a woman carrying deep scars, scars that will never heal as long as she lives. She had been married before, in Germany, and her husband came home wounded from the Russian front.

After he recuperated she accompanied him on the train back to the central point where he was to rejoin his regiment. They were young, barely 19 years old and very much in love. While they were standing in the hallway of the train embracing each other, him with his back to the window, he was shot.

At first she did not realize what had happened, until she felt the full weight of his body in her arms, then saw the blood and started screaming. He died in her arms right there and she was never the same person again. Though she had remarried, moved to England and born her husband two sons, she never did forget the young man whom she had loved with all her heart. I remember her tears when she told us what had happened. Afterwards, the scorn and verbal abuse she endured in England for years, were an easy burden to bear.

She never complained, but on the inside she was a broken spirit.

We are actually glad when our three weeks in Yorkshire are over and look forward to being in London. Eva in particular, since she has not been there, and I because I love the city and know we will have fun. We check into the same youth hostel in Marylebone close to Oxford Street and I basically show my friend all the sights I have visited before.

We are mischievous, the two of us! While visiting
Buckingham Palace we notice that we catch the eye of a
young soldier who is standing guard in one of the Guard
Houses. One of his shoelaces has become untied. Knowing
full well that they are not allowed to talk under their big
headdress with a large strap around their chin almost
covering their mouths, we boldly stand in front of him and
make him aware of his plight. At first he does not even
blink an eye, just stares ahead motionless like he is
supposed to, but we don't give up easily. We ask him if he
wants us to tie his shoelace and finally the young man
cannot stand the sight of two pretty girls teasing him any
longer and mumbles: "go ahead, if you wish." I stoop down,
tie his shoelace and as I do an elderly Englishman,
distinguished looking with Bowler hat and umbrella, for all
I know he could have been a Member of Parliament, stops
and gives me a tongue-lashing like I have never received.
How dare we bother one of the Queen's Guards, how
shamefully disrespectful! I simply turn to him and ask if he
thinks it would be better if the young man were to do his
required march every 10 minutes and trip over his shoelace?
That really infuriates him, since he notices we are
foreigners to boot and he is about to call a Bobby (English
police officer) waving his "brolly" in a threatening manner.

We take one last look at the young man in uniform who
gives us a quick wink with one eye and walk away, while
the old British gentleman is close to cardiac arrest. The
British really do take their traditions a bit far, we decide,
and have a good laugh anyway. It is not that we are being
disrespectful, we are just typical teenagers having a bit of
fun and see no harm in what we did.

One day we arrive back at the youth hostel to change
and I find that my good Sunday coat, which was purchased

just prior to our trip, has been stolen. It is very upsetting to me but I am thankful that Mama had the good foresight to have me take out a travel insurance policy. Mama is very practical and does not trust easily, actually, ever since the War she really does not trust anyone, and that is sometimes a good thing. Gypsies frequently pass through the village and are well known for their thievery, brazenly stealing everything in sight. So at least I will be reimbursed for my coat and I am grateful to have another warm overcoat with me for the return across the icy cold and choppy waters of the British Channel. We visit every sight I saw the previous summer and also spend a lot of time in the British Museum, especially on those very cold and rainy days one gets in England in March. All in all our trip is a big success and two happy young girls return to Cologne. We are full of pleasant memories and interesting experiences.

Since we have mostly spoken English, even with each other, once again there is a big improvement in our conversational skills. It becomes very obvious during the next semester. We are really pulling ahead and feel a great deal closer to our goal.

The next semester passes quickly. I continue to read myself through two English books a week. The assignments are getting increasingly difficult and we spend a lot of time translating articles from the ECONOMIST, Britain's foremost business magazine. Along with that we study British and American literature, a subject I enjoy very much.

Eva, Susanne and I still spend a lot of time together on weekends. I don't particularly care to go to Susanne's house. With four sisters, three of them older and one younger, there is always mayhem at her house; bickering about clothing items or money. Thus we either meet in town or at Eva's.

Mama has gotten worse concerning her obsession with Tante Grete and her fits of depression seem more frequent. By now I am really getting tired of the constant recounting of my parents' war experiences. I am too young, too self-absorbed, to understand the long-term effects that trauma has had on both of my parents and have little understanding or empathy for them. To me they are stories I have heard ever since I can remember and I am sick and tired of listening. "Get on with your lives already," I think quite often, but I don't say it because that would be disrespectful and cause a major argument which I try to avoid by any means. Right now it is most peaceful at Eva's house. She has a younger sister and they share a room, but her parents have made an adorable small study for her in the attic. It is tiny, just enough for book shelves, a small built-in sofa and a coffee table. But it has a skylight and is cozy as can be. The chimney with its old exposed bricks goes right through the study keeping it warm in the winter and creates a charming background for the bookshelves. We spend many hours in this tiny hidden away space, both in serious study as well as in girlish laughter. Eva intends to go to Madrid, Spain, for a year, once she has passed her English exams to become a certified translator. She has a clear talent for the language and has obtained a scholarship at the University of Madrid. Naturally she is very excited about her plans and we spend countless hours discussing how much fun it will be for her. However I will miss her a lot.

My studies progress nicely and I do get to have a social life after all. I have allowed my home life to slip quietly into the background, my thoughts are mostly taken up with affairs concerning the University.

In the spring I once again work at the Trade Fair for the same Company as I did the previous year, plus that August my sister, who is now employed at the local radio and TV station, makes it possible for me to get a job working for one of the editors in the department "The Cultural Word."

I am to fill in for the regular secretary who is on vacation for a month. It is a wonderful opportunity for me. I work in the building right opposite from the Cologne Cathedral. By now I have mastered stenography in German as well as English and my typing is passable. Working at the radio station I soon find out requires "no heavy lifting." They are a fun loving not terribly driven bunch of people and I am given a "Welcome" as well as a month later a "Farewell Party."

Traditionally August in Germany is THE vacation month and work is slow for me, in particular since my boss, a cigar smoking lady in her late thirties with a PHD is pregnant and spends as little time as possible in the office. She mostly works from home and calls in now and then, usually only appearing twice a week for the taping of her weekly radio program which is aired on weekends. The work is easy, pays well and the people I work with are an interesting and eccentric mix of bohemian characters. I believe what they do best is celebrate! Any occasion, no matter how trivial, is cause to throw a party with Koelsch beer flowing freely. If my sister ever complains again about having to work too hard I will tell her just how good she has it. There is no comparison between this job, she too is a secretary, and the demands at the University.

First Love

In September my mother and I will go on vacation to the Italian Riviera where by now both of us have been several times. I look forward to Bella Vista, the hotel I have stayed at before, and I can pay my own way. The weather on the Italian Riviera is quite beautiful in September and the ocean is warm.

I sneak a tiny bikini into my luggage and as luck would have it, on the second day of our stay, while walking along the beach with my mother, I notice a tall, dark-haired young man looking at me intensely. Our eyes catch for a moment and I remember thinking how handsome he is. That afternoon my mother takes a siesta after a magnificent lunch, while I return to the beach. Laying on my beach towel I am reading a book while sunning myself when, all of a sudden, someone sits down next to me and asks me in French whether I speak the language. It is the young man whom I noticed in the morning. Quite obviously, he noticed me as well. We communicate in French since I remember a sufficient amount of words from my days in high school to make myself understood. Before he leaves we arrange to meet at a small café that evening and before the night is over I am in LOVE! For the remainder of my vacation we are inseparable. Having a French mother and an Italian father who owns several boutiques along the Italian Riviera, he himself is a pre-med student. The attraction is mutual and intense, I even get to meet his parents.

I have dated before but this is very different. Aside from the physical attraction, I find him to be an absolutely fascinating person, extremely deep and unlike anyone I have ever met before. We spend hours discussing

159

philosophy and it is him who introduces me to Nietzsche, Kierkegaard, Sartre and Camus.

I perceive a certain depth and melancholy, rare for a young man of 19, which I find enormously seductive and charming. His grandfather, still alive and very old, lives on Cape d'Antibes, the French Riviera, and used to be a famous surgeon who in his youth studied with Madame Curie. I am duly impressed! All this adds to the mystique and the excitement of a first love. Just the thought of him can make my young heart beat faster. When the time comes for me to leave, both of us stand teary-eyed at the railroad station. We have exchanged addresses and promise each other to write as often as possible. One last embrace, I don't even care that my mother is present, one last hot kiss leaving me with the taste of the Gaulloise cigarettes he smokes, and then I board the train bound for Germany, looking out of the window until his motionless form disappears in the distance. Mama seems to know how I feel. She allows me to be dreamy-eyed and quiet during the long ride back.

Arriving in Germany I throw myself even more into my studies and, like promised, love letters begin to travel back and forth on a regular basis. I virtually live for the days when I return from the University and find a letter by my dinner plate with the by now familiar handwriting. While I still socialize with the Dance Troupe, performing here and there for money, I stop dating entirely and when not occupied with my studies, I am busy improving my knowledge of French. Now that it has become the language of love, I seem to have a much easier time embracing French.

Roger does not speak any German or English, however he is totally bilingual in French and Italian, enjoys dual citizenship and carries both, a French and an Italian passport.

There is an occurrence during one of my college classes that bothers me a great deal and is to me representative of that part of the German character which I despise.

At this point the "German Economic Miracle" under Erhard has reached a new level and a lot of Italian immigrant workers are being brought into the country. They take over the type of low-paying jobs, Germans do not want to do any longer, such as sanitation workers, waiters in restaurants, street sweepers etc. They are being looked down upon as second class citizens and the derogatory expression "Itakker" is coined.

Being fortunate in that my father's occupation makes it possible for me to travel a great deal due to my free railroad tickets, I have been exposed to more travel than a lot of other post-war Germans, and I have learned early to respect and appreciate each culture for its own distinctive qualities. Thus when one of my professors, an elderly man, strangely enough Jewish, asks me in front of the entire student body where I spent my vacation, followed by the inappropriate question if I have an "Itakker" boyfriend now, there is a lot of laughter at my expense and I am furious inside. "If you were only half as intelligent as my boyfriend," I think to myself, "you certainly would not exhibit such despicable prejudice." It particularly galls me that he is Jewish, since I would have thought if anybody would not show prejudice, it would certainly come from the ranks of the few surviving Jews in Germany. They can laugh all they want. I know that dating someone from a different nationality is certainly nothing to be ashamed of, in particular when that someone attends medical school. However, that remark ridiculing me in front of all my friends is not easily forgotten, and when the professor dies the following year I don't miss him in the least.

Meanwhile the Christmas break is approaching and I will be off for at least a week.

To my great delight I receive a letter asking if it is possible for me to return to the Italian Riviera for the New Year's celebration and my parents actually allow me to go.

Somehow though, something goes array with the mail and I do not hear from Roger prior to Christmas, leaving me in a very somber and despondent mood. I remember moping around on Christmas Day and my father telling me not to be too disappointed.

"When the right man enters your life you will know it," he assures me, but that is of little consolation. Consequently I make alternative plans for New Years with my girl friends, that is until later during the week a telegram arrives with the words I long to hear: Je t'attends! (I am waiting for you) A telegram is dispatched the next day by me informing him of the time of my arrival and two evenings later I board the train headed for Ventimiglia with Mama standing at the platform seeing me off, probably living through me vicariously. There is a certain smile on her face which I have never seen before.

After the long train ride through the Alps where heavy snow has fallen, I finally arrive the next day in the early afternoon. There I experience balmy sunshine with blossoming flowers, palm trees and the blue Mediterranean shimmering like a precious opal. Roger is anxiously waiting for me on the platform and takes me to a small hotel near his home, where I will stay for the coming week. This is a magical time for both of us. I am invited to his parent's house on numerous occasions. They truly like me, especially his mother, although I overhear his father making a comment that true, I am a pretty and smart girl, but much too skinny. The family tries to correct this "flaw" within one week, feeding me as much as they can stuff into me. Roger and I spend long days and evenings together lost in deep conversations and each others eyes. I enjoy the most wonderful and happy New Year's Eve party, arranged especially in my honor.

The usually crowded tourist town is nearly empty. Other than the native inhabitants I must be the only visitor and one of my boyfriend's College pals who has a car, takes us way up into the mountains lining the coast and which, at this time of year, are completely snowed in. It is quite an experience to go within one hour from temperatures in the low 70's to a small restaurant literally buried in snow, where we stop for a cup of coffee. It is all so very exciting and foreign. Most nights I go to sleep hearing the sound of flutes and their strange song, played by the shepherds who descend from the mountains in an ancient tradition. They play their instruments and receive special gifts for the holidays. It is said they bring good luck to the town's people and so are amply rewarded for the beautiful tunes they play. Roger and I are falling in love deeper with every moment we spend together and the physical attraction grows more and more intense. The chemistry between us is intoxicating and something I have never experienced before. Were it not for the fear of an unwanted pregnancy which would not be welcomed by either one of us, it would be easy to give in to our feelings and throw caution to the wind. But both of us have plans for the future and, though difficult, we show restraint. However, I extract the promise from him to come and visit me the following spring. His family has relatives in Paris which he is supposed to visit during spring break and after that he will come to Cologne to see me. Again we part, but this time he accompanies me as far as Genoa. After yet another tearful good-bye I am left alone returning to Germany and resuming my studies.

In a way this long distance romance serves both of us well. There is a real incentive to study diligently and we wait eagerly for each other's letters. I think his parents are quite aware of the fact that I am not distracting him. On the contrary, with the reward of allowing him to see me he takes his studies more serious than before. Actually he never wanted to study medicine and was more interested in philosophy, but his parents are strict and determined he follow in the footsteps of his grandfather, whether he likes it or not.

Adventures

Early on that spring there is the opportunity for me to participate in a trip across England with a group of fellow students. Having worked once again at the Bath and Kitchen Fair, I have accumulated enough money to go.

The group of students mostly consists of young girls, there are only two male participants, and the accompanying professor who arranges the trip is one of our favorites. We all adore him from afar but after my previous experience with "teachers" I am cautious regarding the occasional compliments I receive from him.

He is a wonderful professor and knows how to motivate his students well.

The trip should be a lot of fun since we plan to spend ten days in the Lake District, Poets' Corner, then visit Oxford, Blenheim Place, Eaton and Windsor Castle. The last four days will be spent in London. By now I am quite familiar with the route, the train ride from Cologne to Oostend and the subsequent crossing by ferry to Dover. Susanne travels with us. This is the first time for her in England and travelling with this group is truly a lot of fun. It helps that we all get along well. Once we arrive at our first destination, the English Lake District, we stay at various youth hostels, some of them renovated old castles. Since we are of legal drinking age a nightly stop at the local pubs becomes a routine. The trip is full of fun, laughter and we are terribly mischievous, especially Susanne and I. We are supposed to hike through the Lake District but on one of the earliest hikes Susanne, myself and the two male students fall way behind. It is a hot day, and just for fun we stick out our thumbs. To our great surprise the first car, driven by a middle-aged couple, stops and takes the four of us to our destination, a pub and restaurant high up in the hills. We duck when passing the professor and the rest of the students who arrive two hours later at the restaurant in a state of total exhaustion, astounded to find us there having lunch with a cool pint of ale. At first we are reluctant to tell the professor how we got there so fast but eventually we fess up and tell him we hitchhiked. After some general discussion of the subject it is decided unanimously, that with the meager financial means at our disposal we can see a lot more of the country if we were to hitchhike in groups of three for safety reasons, provided that we will not tell anybody about our adventure, because the professor is taking a huge risk in allowing us to do so. We make the solemn vow never to divulge our secret and immediately begin to make plans for our wider exploration of the area. This is an exciting prospect. Instead of having to confine ourselves we can travel all the way up to the Scottish border. We hitchhike in groups of three up north, meet up in Carlisle and from there we take the next trip to the Hadrian's Wall. We walk on the ancient Roman wall which is the dividing line between Britain and Scotland. Finding the ruins of an old Roman bath we try to imagine what it used to look like when the Romans occupied Britain or Gaul as they called this furthest northerly outpost of the Roman Empire.

Another day we hitchhike to the famous seaside resort or Morecamb.

Susanne and I, as well as another girl, are lucky enough to hitch a ride in a huge American convertible, driven by a handsome young Englishman. The day is warm and we feel joyous, free and adventurous. Once in Morecamb, we meet with the others of our group for lunch, then Susanne and I take a walk along the deserted beach once in a while

166

dipping our feet into the icy-cold waters of the Atlantic. On other days we stay in the Lake District itself, row a boat on Lake Windemere and take some further hikes through the hills. In June the Lake District is very colorful due to an abundance of rhododendron bushes which are in full bloom. They are stunningly beautiful and we have never seen them in such large numbers or so huge in size. One of the hikes takes us to an interesting discovery, a small Stonehenge on a windswept hill. Every night we end the evening at the local pub in Keswick where we mingle with students from other parts of Europe. On one of our drives from Keswick Susanne and I hitch a ride to the Youth Hostel with a retired teacher who has made a home for herself in an old shepherd's cottage on the shores of Lake Derwentwater. A kindly lady, she enjoys our company and asks us to join her for a cup of tea. We gladly accept since we are intrigued by her charming home. Once inside, both Susanne and I look at each each other and we are both thinking the same thought: we want to live here!

The old shepherd's cottage, which had fallen into disrepair, has been transformed into the most charming and cozy home either one of us has ever seen. The stone walls have been preserved and the house basically consists of a great-room, a beautiful staircase leading up to a bedroom-loft and a full bath. The rear of the cottage has been opened up with windows and a large glass door, giving a full sweeping view of the lake and the surrounding mountains. A flagstone patio, slightly overgrown with moss and occasionally beautified with high-stemmed roses in full bloom, leads to the edge of the lake itself. We have our tea on the patio and chat about her life as a teacher, while she has many questions for us regarding our plans for the future. What a lovely lady and what a charming retirement home she has created for herself . The memory of that afternoon, though the event will seem rather trivial to most people our age, stays with me. The entire setting can be summed up in one word: SERENITY.

Eventually we have to leave because we have to be at the Youth Hostel housed in a huge old mansion across expansive lawns from the shepherd's cottage.

We are late and in order not to upset the strict warden we pull another prank and throw some pebbles at our window on the second floor, asking one of our friends to come down and unlock the side door. Unseen we sneak in and tell the others about our wonderful discovery.

Soon our time in the Lake District is over, and instead of taking the train back we decide to hitchhike, this time with our luggage, agreeing to meet up in the center of Birmingham between 1p.m. and 2 p.m. Susanne, Otto and I hitch a ride on a lorry, taking turns sitting on the hot engine-cover. It is very uncomfortable and we are glad to reach Birmingham, wait around for the others and then head on to the outskirts of Oxford. Staying at another Youth Hostel there, we visit Eaton, Windsor Castle and on the following day check into a place in Oxford itself. This is graduation time and we see many young men in their long graduation robes driving fancy sports cars. The grounds around the colleges are covered with elaborate tents for the graduation ceremonies and the entire town is a beehive of activities. We admire the architecture of Christopher Wren and achieving access to some of the college buildings, we realize that this is where the British elite, the world elite is raised. How I wish I could study here! I would love to absorb as much knowledge as possible on this ancient campus and mingle with the interesting people from all over the world attending classes here.

Actually I am not intimidated. I feel at home here, much like I feel at home in any other place I have had the good fortune to visit. The only place I don't seem to feel at home is in my own town in my native country. There are many times I wonder why, because it cannot only be caused by my dysfunctional home life.

Something is pulling at the very core of me, crying out for the freedom to explore and experience other places, people and cultures. The Tumbleweed is maturing at a faster rate than ever before, yet the course it will take is still a mystery to me. All I am acutely aware of is this intense longing I feel.

The final days of our trip take us to a four-day stay in London, a city which I know quite well by now. There are some sites we have to visit as a group of students, however a good amount of time we are left to explore on our own.

One of the funniest experiences happens to be a visit to the Houses of Parliament which is in session and where we can watch the process of government from the Visitor's Gallery. It is a madhouse, Members of Parliament jumping up and shouting at each other, even insults fly across the room but everyone, including the Speaker, seems to have a jolly good time. What a difference from the solemn hearings in the Bundestag, at least the members show a sense of humor. How much governing is actually taking place is anyone's guess. I take Susanne to some of my favorite places.

Mini-skirts are getting shorter and shorter, and while in London we roll up our skirts, buy the latest fashion in shoe-wear and a pair of cool shades. Not that one needs them much in England, but walking along Oxford Street, Piccadilly Circus and Carnaby Street we feel that we fit right in.

169

The trip to England is a huge success. We have seen so much more than we ever anticipated and the professor's secret is safe with us. Indeed, we are very grateful to him. He too is pleased because nobody disappointed him.

The Dean of the Language School never finds out!

A week later my boyfriend arrives from Paris and I pick him up at the Cologne Railroad Station. We spend the afternoon in Cologne visiting some sites and then head for the suburbs where I have made reservations for him at a small hotel. He did not want to stay at my house, even though he was invited but, as luck would have it for me, he falls ill that first night and I have to take him to our family physician and then insist he move out of the hotel and come home with me. So I have my wish, Roger all to myself in my own house. Unfortunately I don't have vacation but have to attend classes and there are quite a few tests during his stay. For once I really don't study that hard yet I do better in my test scores than ever before. That is what being in love can accomplish. I am deliriously happy for the next two weeks and anxious to show him what life in my country is all about. Naturally, he does not care for the German climate but we have a wonderful time and, I am glad to say, that my parents refrain from their usual hostility towards each other. As a matter of fact, I think they are beginning to like Roger.

I introduce him to my friends, take him to a rehearsal of our dance troupe and a lot of time is spent at the Café Paris with other students. Here he can smoke his Gaulloise cigarettes while involved in deep philosophical discussions, his favorite topic and I often think what a wonderful philosophy professor he would make. But his parents insist he become a doctor and follow in the footsteps of his grandfather. When we are alone and take long walks in the park I no longer resist his roving hands which every time we are together seem to be getting bolder. His passionate kisses can cause my knees to buckle and I savor every moment we have to the fullest.

When the time comes for him to return I am saddened but by now it is almost July and we will see each other again for the entire month of September.

August is spent studying because the State Examination to become a Certified Translator will take place in October. For once we are having beautiful summer weather and Eva spends a lot of time at my house where we study outside in the garden. She will take her State Exam and is by now already enrolled at the University of Madrid, where she will stay for a year.

Between studies and work in August time passes quickly, and once again I find myself going South to the Riviera in the company of my mother. I would rather have gone by myself, but this time we are not staying at Bella Vista up on the mountain but right in town, which makes it easy to reach the beach and my love. As always, when one is happy, time seems to fly by. I am asked to bring Mama along to some of the family dinners I am invited to. Although there is the language barrier, she seems to have a good time. One night after dinner at Roger's aunt's house we walk home and are surprised by his parents taking my mother back to the hotel. Roger and I are standing on the sidewalk locked in a passionate embrace, kissing. Tooting the horn they are laughing and joking about the love birds. They understand how we feel about each other. While there we already make plans for my return during Christmas vacation. Our love deepens and remains strong though there are thousands of miles between us. As far as the families are concerned, his parents could not be more pleased, and my parents have accepted the fact, that in order to talk to my boyfriend, they need me to translate. After a blissful time once again I find myself at the train station crying my eyes out. However, I know I will be back in December and that makes the separation bearable. I will also be very busy that fall since we are going for our translator's State Examination, which will require my full attention and concentration.

Upon our return and prior to the examination I stay at Eva's house since her parents are on vacation. Plus the tension and discourse have again settled over my own home. The arguments are fierce and vicious, there are weekends when I already wake up hearing them scream at each other in the morning. I stick my head under the covers and pray for the time to come when I will be able to leave all this behind. Mama is getting worse in her accusations of Tante Grete. Once again the ugly scenario I remember so well from the incident with my grandparents repeats itself. I am told not to speak to Tante Grete any longer, a command I ignore when I know my mother is not at home, because I have no intention of having my relationship with Tante

Grete terminated. So I escape to Eva's house! We study like mad and go for the State Exam, waiting anxiously for the results which will be known within a week's time. While we are in a state of limbo we spend long hours discussing Eva's imminent departure for Madrid after the results are disclosed and Susanne joins us on occasion. She has decided to end her studies at the translator stage and already found a job with the Australian Consulate in Cologne. This is a time in Australia where immigrants are badly needed and it will be Susanne's job to process applications from all over Europe, arrange for the visas and with her boss accompany groups of immigrants to Great Britain, where in Southampton they are placed on ships and transported to Sydney. It sounds very exciting to me but I have decided to go as far as I can in my education and become an interpreter. This will require two more semesters of extensive studies focussed strictly on simultaneous and consecutive interpreting.

Anxiously Eva and I await the results and, since neither one of us has a telephone, we go to the nearest public phone booth a week later to find out if we passed. We did! Both of us, with good grades to boot. We are ecstatic.

We are so happy that we go to the nearest liquor store and buy two cheap bottles of red wine, which we start to drink as soon as we get home. All I remember is sitting under her parents' living room table, the latest songs from the BEATLES blaring and us singing along. I do not tolerate alcohol very well and end the night by throwing up. Both of us experience a rude awakening in the morning and looking at each other bleary-eyed we wonder if we look as badly as we feel. I am positive we do! My stomach is doing somersaults and my head is pounding, whether I leave it on the pillow or get up. So we stay in bed, take two aspirin and just wait until the enormous hangover passes. We promise each other never to do this again! It just is not worth feeling this miserable. However, we passed the State Exams and are entitled to call ourselves State Certified Translators.

Within a month Eva leaves for Spain, Susanne who likewise passed, begins her employment with the Australian Consulate and I return to classes at the University.

Very few students make it all the way. The class size has shrunk to less than a dozen students and I have to find new companions. There is Regine and Monika, who during the next year will become good friends. Monika lives in Cologne proper in a tiny student apartment, since her home is in the Eiffel Mountains, the vicinity of the Nuernburgring, where her mother and older brother run a small hotel. Even though Monika's apartment is tiny, the situation at my home has become so unbearable again, that quite often I stay at her place and we study together. The apartment is your typical student attic, a tiny garret under the eaves and a shared bathroom with other students who are renting there. However, it provides a safe haven for studying and light-heartedness. While there, I am able to detach myself and be cheerful and carefree. Many a morning Monika goes down to get some fresh rolls for breakfast while I am still in bed, wanting to sleep in. Her ultimate weapon to get me out of bed is threatening to go back to sleep herself, which would make me responsible for her missing class and I cannot do that. Reluctantly I get up and we take the trolley to the University. This year we have a new professor teaching Economics. He is a bachelor and rather timid. By now I have become very precocious. After all the traveling and performing on stage I have finally been able to leave the shy ME behind. Sensing that this new professor is vulnerable to the charms of a young female student in a mini-skirt and mini-sweater, I take advantage of the situation shamelessly.

Much to my fellow students' delight I succeed within minutes of his entering the lecture hall in getting him into a totally flustered state of mind, simply by dropping my pen in a certain strategic spot near my seat. He turns beet-red, being torn between behaving like a gentleman picking up the pen, while in the process having to get very close to the portion of my legs not covered by my mini-skirt, or ignoring the matter completely. This throws the poor man into emotional turmoil so much so that quite often he looses his train of thought. Usually the polite gentleman wins out and subdued snickering can be heard throughout the room.

There are other pranks we play. One day we all decide to take his lecture "off" and leave a message on the blackboard saying:

"Come join us at the pub around the corner!" We wait for him but he never shows up.

Instead, upon our return, we find him sitting at his desk in an empty lecture-hall, not even having the courage to chastise us. He was afraid the Dean would find out that he was not in control and this time we truly feel sorry for him. Actually, we are ashamed of ourselves and decide as a group to treat him in a kinder fashion. He is a good professor. His lectures, though extremely boring, are well prepared and his grading is fair.

Roger pays me a surprise visit late in the fall, traveling with two fellow student friends who are visiting their girl friends in Holland and in Germany.

They stay in a hotel nearby and we rekindle the flame of our young love.

There is just never enough time it seems. But then again that very fact only heightens the passion we feel for each other and the time we do spend together is one of great intensity, filled with the mutual expression of love and desire.

This love is sustained by the weekly letters. Meanwhile I have entire stacks of them, tied together neatly with pink ribbons. I always perfume my letters prior to dispatching them, having noticed how fragrances can intensify the emotions.

Eva meanwhile has settled into the University of Madrid and found the love of her life. These are the years of civil unrest in opposition to General Franco and her boyfriend is a key-member of the "Falanche," the student movement which is responsible for the majority of demonstrations and unrest in the country. Eva herself is caught up in the political action and her boyfriend even ends up in jail a few times for his part in the anti-Franco movement. Her letters are exciting to read. Through the detailed accounts of her life in Spain I get to travel with her all over the country, partake in the running of the bulls in Pamplona, see Andalucia all the way up to the Portuguese border and travel back along the Atlantic coast. She travels a lot, passionately in love with a man who she knows will never be hers' because his political cause takes priority over everything else.

But then there is always hope in a young girl's heart when she is in love! Eva is doing very well at the University and really likes everything about her life in Spain. These are exciting times for both of us, but they are also times fraught with angst and intense work towards our final professional goals.

Interpreting is very difficult and stressful. We learn a special way of taking notes for consecutive interpretations, i.e. when someone holds a speech we take notes and then interpret an entire paragraph. The other type, simultaneous interpreting, is even more stressful. We practice in a language laboratory with headphones like they have at the UN, listening to speeches by Martin Luther King, Malcom X, John F. Kennedy or Robert Kennedy. Mostly the material is of a political or economic nature. While listening we interpret at the same time into a microphone, and when the professor cuts in a red light flashes. I usually cover the light with my hand, because I find I get distracted and loose my train of thought once I see the red light go on. This is the highest level of language proficiency and requires an enormous amount of concentration skills. There are certain tricks we learn during these last two semesters which come in handy. Given the intensity of my studies this period leaves very little time for a social life and so it is just as well that my boyfriend lives so far away.

Unfortunately Roger has not done well in his studies and will have to attend intercession. This means that we will not be able to see each other during the Christmas break, leaving me lonely and depressed. A telephone call is simply not sufficient, I crave his loving touch so badly. But it will simply have to wait until later.

During the spring break Monika informs me that she will have her mother's car for two weeks and asks me if I am interested in travelling with her through France. Am I interested? Of course I am! I am packed and on my way as soon as possible. It is a perfect time to run away to the South of France. We cross over the border at Strasbourg, laughing and anticipating what a good time we will have. We spend the first night in Chalon-sur-Saone, somewhere between Dijon and Lyon, where we treat ourselves to exquisite French dining and ONE glass of red wine. The next day we push on further down the Rhone Valley, stop at

Lyon for lunch and sight seeing. Then we get back into the car and as we get further south there is a marked increase in temperature. By the time we approach Avignon the peach trees are in full bloom and we feel like we have escaped the German winter blues! Avignon is a very special place, not only because of its historic past as the home of the second Pope during some darker times of the Catholic faith, nor because of the renowned Pont d'Avignon, a bridge over the Rhone River that was never completed, but for its atmosphere. Once in Avignon, it is clear that the south of France has been reached and this fact is well reflected in the population. They are of a cheerful, open and easy-going nature like most people in southern Europe. Likewise the accent of the Provence begins to seep into the language which is very charming.

We wish we could linger in Avignon but we only have one day planned into our tight schedule, just enough time to visit the important sites and attractions. The next morning we allow ourselves to be treated to breakfast in bed by the friendly innkeeper's wife; a common practice in France which I find to be very civilized. There is nothing like waking up to a tray of café au lait and fresh croissants. On our way to Marseilles we take a little detour to Nimes, in order to see the famous Roman Aqueduct. On a beautiful day such as this we slowly start to shed our winter clothes and in summer outfits take a walk on top of the ancient structure. The Pont du Gare is very impressive and certainly worth visiting.

Later in the afternoon we arrive in Marseilles, and since our budget is limited, I always seem to travel on a shoe-string, we take a small room in an inexpensive hotel close to the old harbor. Marseilles is a beautiful city with a very foreign flavor due to the fact that a large part of the population is of Arabic descend. From our hotel window we can see the boats bobbing in the Boat Basin as well as the Cathedral of Notre Dame de la Guarde, perched on top of a mountain. We dine in a small restaurant on the Cannebierre, Marseilles' main avenue, and allow ourselves to be filled with a delightful mixture of French and Arabic sounds. The next day we go and explore.

We know that Marseilles has a rather high crime rate and it already has a bad reputation for drug-trafficking, but if there is any danger, we are totally unaware. From the top of the cathedral which we reach by cable car, we enjoy the view of the entire bustling city, sprawled out way below us along the coast of the deep blue Mediterranean. Unfortunately we are again pressed for time and though we would have liked to stay a while longer, spending endless hours sitting in a café on the Cannebierre "people-watching," we are close to our final goal now: the incomparable Cote d'Azure. I have been to Monaco during previous trips to Italy, but then I had approached it from the Italian Riviera. This time we take the entire coast line to visit St. Tropez, Cannes, Nice and all those classy resorts of the rich and famous. By now the mimosa trees are in full bloom and we see palm trees, oleander and even the plain green grass is such a joy after a dreary winter.

An entire afternoon is devoted to St. Tropez, eating at a sinfully expensive restaurant, but we spend only a very brief time in Toulon. Somehow I have always liked tourist resorts off-season and this is no exception. In early spring hardly anybody is here, while in August one would be hard-pressed to find a spot to park or on any beach.

Cannes is foggy, very foggy. We are most interested in the old part of the city, the winding streets with the definite Arabic influence leading us to a point from which the

179

Mediterranean lies at our feet. At night we sit in a sidewalk café along the Croisette, the main promenade. For the longest time we simply cannot figure out why these beautiful young girls are riding up and down the promenade in their fancy sports cars until finally it dawns on us, that they are the local prostitutes out there on business. We in turn start looking for an inexpensive hotel late at night, finally locate one, only to wake up in the morning to find ourselves in the midst of the red-light district. Quite a novel and unusual experience, one we will not easily forget and only adds to the adventure of the trip.

From Cannes Monika wants to go straight to Nice but I insist we stop off at Antibes. Roger has told me a lot about Cap d'Antibes since his Grandpa, the famous and much decorated surgeon, has retired there. The Cape juts out between Cannes and Nice. Many people pass by without realizing what they are missing by not taking a little detour. The side facing the harbor of Cannes, Juan les Pins, famous for the fast life of the Disco-crowd is nice, but it is the old town of Antibes facing Nice which becomes precious to me.

Surrounded by Les Ramparts, the ancient Moorish walls, the narrow streets wind their way through the town in the most charming fashion. Windows adorned with flower boxes overflow with fragrant blossoms. When sitting on the wall surrounding the historic area I can loose myself for hours just allowing my eyes to drift past the blue sea towards the snow-capped Alps Maritime in the distance. What a lovely place to linger and dream of love, of youth and being carefree. During our stay in Antibes we venture out in our bikinis onto a rock outcropping catching the early spring rays of the sun.

They are warm enough for sunbathing but of such intensity, that Monika contracts sun-poisoning and is confined to the hotel room with a swollen face for three days. Since I have always been a firm believer in exploring a location on foot, I spend this time walking around Antibes. Never in my life have I seen a more beautiful place. Why couldn't I have been born here?

Like magic the truly ancient stone walls surrounding "old" Antibes draw me back again and again, because northern eyes are not accustomed to such beauty.

There is another interesting aspect to strolling on the Ramparts. I can watch the old men play "boule," the favorite regional past time of French men. A simple but skilful game, generating much animated discussion and laughter among the mostly older players.

Once Monika has recovered we go on to visit Nice and Monaco but neither one has the attraction so unique to Antibes. Basically Nice is just another big city and Monaco is terribly congested. Shortly thereafter we already have to think of our departure, and we make our way back through

Vallauris, where the streets are lined with pottery, and Grasse, the "French Perfume Factory."

We climb higher and higher through the Alps, soon reaching snow. It almost seems impossible that just the day before we basked in the sunshine wearing our bikinis. Our last stop is Grenoble, where we spend our last Francs on a farewell dinner and fine wine. On the way back to Germany we are hit by a snow storm in the region of Alsace-Lorraine and the weather, as well as our mood, get progressively worse. A beautiful and adventurous two week journey, undertaken by two young girls who like to explore, comes to an end. Before we realize it we are back in College for the final stretch.

While I am still quite unaware of the existence and name of a certain desert plant, the Tumbleweed in me has almost reached maturity.

Achieving my goal

And so we go back to serious work in our studies. The interpretation practices in the language lab become more and more demanding from week to week as do the exercises in consecutive interpreting. These specialized skills are extremely stressful but I handle them. Intermittently we have quite a bit of fun with the professors. We have come to respect each other, after all, very few students make it to this point, and since most of the professors are not much older than in their mid-to late thirties, the gap between us has shrunken considerably. We even invite them to our parties given by a few of my fellow students and they actually attend. The head of the Department at this point is the very professor whom I annoyed by not showing up for class on time on my very first day as a student. But he has long since forgiven me and there is a relationship of mutual respect. I want to do well in his classes because I hate to notice any type of disapproval coming from him. At the same time he obviously has come to like me and is pleased when I do well. All of us consider him a very "eligible bachelor" although it is well known that he is divorced from a former student of his and the father of a son. He still drives his racy red Porsche sports car and his appearance, thin and tall with wild hair wearing the typical "Tweed jacket – Corduroy slacks professor uniform" is much admired, turning the heads of all female students.

Shortly before summer break my friend Regina and I are the last to leave the auditorium when he asks us where we intend to go for the summer. "The South of France," we answer in unison, because that is what our plans are. I have told Regina just how beautiful Cap d'Antibes is and we have decided to go there for three weeks. "France? But you are majoring in English! What are you going to be doing in the South of France?" The professor is obviously perplexed. "Study at the beach," we say, "what else?" Naturally I have made plans to meet up with Roger there, who will be staying at his grandfather's villa. The professor asks us for the dates we will be there and then tells us that he might stop by. He has not made firm travel plans yet and I tell him about the trip I took with Monika that spring, how I simply fell in love with the old part of Antibes. We never thought he would be serious about coming to see us however, after our return, he tells us that he was there and looked for us on all the different beaches. Too bad he was not able to find us.

Roger comes as promised and his stay becomes the highlight of the summer for me, since for the first time he finally says the words I have been waiting for so long: "Je t'aime." (I love you.) While he has showered me with many compliments and told me in the past I made him happy, these words were never spoken. While both of us know that there is a long time until he can make an honest commitment, we promise to wait for each other and officially consider ourselves engaged. These are heady times for me and strangely enough, Regina herself meets the man she will marry three years later. He is a young Frenchman from Paris, a printer by trade and a committed socialist. We double date frequently and the discussions that take place are centered around different philosophies and political discourse. The Vietnam War is in full swing, a never ending subject in many conversations.

One day, while walking through town by myself, I am approached by a young American deserter who is intensely distraught and needs someone to talk to. He was stationed in Germany, very much in love with a young German girl, and when he received his notification to leave for Vietnam he panicked. The young soldier deserted in the middle of the night, made his way to the South of France, from where he intends to take a ship to Canada out of Marseilles or Toulon. He would like me to let his girl friend know that he loves her and that she will hear from him later. I take down her name and address, promising to write her a letter to inform her of his whereabouts and of the fact, that while he has left Germany, he has no intention of leaving her. When the young man looses himself in a crowd his mind is somewhat more at ease and I am glad I can help. That war in Vietnam is so very wrong. Since I know about war first-hand I am happy the young American deserter chose me to carry out this very personal mission.

The final semester is difficult in many ways. Not only have the pressures in College increased and all my time is taken up by studies trying to get the best grade I can achieve, but my home life has taken on a strange twist.

Mama in her obsessive behavior has actually thrown Tante Grete out. My beloved aunt is forced to move in a hurry. I do not understand what is happening to my mother. She has convinced herself that her own sister has turned against her, and she has subjected Tante Grete, who has been so loyal all these years, to various humiliations I find abhorrent. While Tante Grete has rented for years the renovated "shack" we used to live in, paying for the renovation plus rent and utilities, she used to have access to the bathroom in the new house since the old outhouse is a mere distant memory. Mama took her keys to the house away and while Tante Grete has had water in her little kitchen, there were no bathroom facilities. I will never understand what obsessed my mother to be so cruel.

Sometimes she has explosive fits of rage directed towards her own sister, my father, ...the entire world and I am seriously beginning to question her sanity. Her strange behavior scares me. Tante Grete leaves moving to an old ruin in the center of Cologne, and a year goes by before I can muster the courage to seek her out. Once Tante Grete is gone my mother's entire fury and compulsive/obsessive behavior is aimed at my father full force.

As I am getting closer to my State Examination and the pressure is mounting, it becomes increasingly difficult to put up with the additional stress at home. The only thing that preserves my own sanity are Roger's letters which arrive like clockwork. When they do, I have a good day! I retreat to my room, close the door and only go downstairs for meals that are eaten in complete silence. About two weeks prior to the final exam I bring Monika home to study at my house when Mama starts ranting and raving about the injustices she has suffered due to others in her life. She loves to play the "blame game" in order to manipulate others. Finally I cannot take it any longer. I virtually explode with anger, pack my clothes and leave with Monika. For the time being I move in with her. I cry! I am angry! I do not understand why my life has to be in such constant turmoil. Other families do not live like that. And now it makes me particularly angry when it comes to the ultimate assignment of blame.

Had it not been for me, my mother would have never married my father.

I am so sick and tired of hearing that. "How can I be to blame, "I ask myself," how unfair!" "Why don't they finally take responsibility for their own lives? I did not ask to be born." So I leave with Mama's harsh words following me as I walk out the door: she does not care if she ever sees me again.

Since the finals are only two weeks away I take some money I have saved out of my bank account in order to contribute to Monika's expenses. It is generous of her to allow me to stay with her in the tiny apartment, but then again we study well together and so this arrangement benefits us both. The only thing I miss are the letters from Roger. But first things first.

Only eight students take the State Examination to become Certified Interpreters that semester. At first there are the written examinations, consisting of a spelling test with words that in the future we shall never use again, such as "zephyr", next there is a written composition with a different subject for every student.

187

I am asked for a dissertation on the question: "There have always been wars – do you personally believe there always will be wars in the future?" "How very appropriate," I think. Then we are questioned on economic and political subjects. The really stressful part comes last; facing the Board of State Examiners for the verbal part.

Our nerves are frazzled as we are being called in one by one, asked to sit down and the examination begins. To my amazement I hold up well under the extreme pressure and leave the room feeling I have done my very best and probably passed.

The results are announced the same day, the Diplomas are singed, sealed and handed out by the Head State Examiner. He calls each student individually, shakes our hands and congratulates us on our achievements. I have done well and have passed with a B plus. I never knew anybody who passed with an A. While I am relieved and happy to have achieved my goal, finishing my education with such a good grade, by the end of the day the stress produces a migraine of gigantic proportions which I know by now will last for days. Since Monika is leaving for home I pack my bags and find refuge at my sister's apartment, where I go straight to bed in a darkened room, trying to cope with the excruciating pain in my head and the terrible nausea. Since my sister also suffers from migraines ever so often, she understands and keeps the baby quiet. I lie in the baby's room on the couch for days sick to my stomach and my head hurting so badly that I feel I shall die if I don't get any relief soon.

On the third day my father shows up. Apparently my sister contacted him to let him he know where I am. Like a beaten puppy he sits next to me and begs me to come home. I tell him what Mama said. He tries to convince me that she did not mean it but I don't believe him. He tells me that she is going through her change of life and is having a hard time at it; that I should forgive her and come home. How do you forgive a person whom you love but who removes much loved relatives from your life in such a cruel fashion?

I don't know how to do that and I struggle with the ambiguity of my feelings.

My mother loves me, I do not doubt that, but she has a very strange way of expressing her love at times.

Eventually I give in, pack my belongings in my suitcase and take the bus home. I am not welcomed with open arms. Consequently I go straight to my room and back to bed until finally the pain subsides and I begin to feel human again.

After this incidence things at home are never the same again. I had not thought they could get worse but gradually they do, to the point where I must leave in order to survive. However, first I have to find employment and I waste little time looking for a position in my field of expertise.

My resume goes out to companies I find in the employment section of the Frankfurter Allgemeine, one of Germany's best newspapers, and I receive an offer from a company located in Munich, as well as one from an insurance company in Cologne. I am torn. I would love to go to Munich but, never having lived away from home, at this point I am intimidated by the process of finding my own apartment, wondering if my starting salary will cover my expenses. I want to move out desperately and know that eventually I will, but my father and mother promise me to keep a more peaceful home life. It is their opinion that I should stay for a while longer. Thus I decide to interview for the job offered in Cologne. In retrospect I believe they are apprehensive of my moving out, since then they will have to face each other directly without me acting as a lightening rod. The company in Munich is willing to hire me right on the spot due to my credentials and my resume, offering me a higher than expected starting salary. Interviewing with the insurance company in Cologne I am asked to translate a document. I get to meet my future boss, the chairman of all the foreign offices, and I am duly impressed by his luxurious and spacious office as well as the fact that he has two secretaries.

When presenting my diploma to him, something I am very proud of, he totally disregards it asking me instead what my father does." What does it matter," I think," I should be judged on my own accomplishment." I can see that once I tell him my father works for the railroad, he immediately places me into a certain class. That is the way the system works. Once working class it is virtually impossible to get out of it. I deeply resent this fact and always will. The next day I receive a call back that they would like to hire me at a comparable salary as the company in Munich. However they also offer fantastic benefits, six weeks vacation plus 14 and one-third salaries per year. I am confused, very much so, but ultimately I decide to take the position, thinking that the experience will be beneficial and in another year I can easily look elsewhere.

When I go to sign my employment contract they want me to start right away but I stipulate that I must have 10 days off during the Christmas Holidays, because I have already made plans to meet Roger. Although they don't like my request, they give in because I let them know that I can start immediately on November 1st, otherwise I will have to take the offer from the company in Munich.

Once again I have a long commute, starting at 8a.m. with a 30 minute break for lunch, and my workday ends at

5p.m. That entails taking a bus, and two trolleys which take me to the business district in the heart of the city. I am sharing the office with another young woman who translates and interprets French as well as Dutch. The office itself is located in the prestigious complex housing the offices of all the Board Members, and the surroundings are plush to say the least. My desk for instance is mahogany, the walls Italian marble, the floors covered by plush gold-colored carpeting.

There is a large glass door leading out into the hallway adorned with little golden crowns and the window looks out into the beautifully landscaped courtyard gardens. The office is truly luxurious and my sophisticated co-worker, just a few years my senior, is a very attractive married young woman. She treats me well. German formality being what it is, I am addressed as "Fraeulein" (Miss) while I have to address her as "Frau"(Mrs.) and that will not change until I leave, since it is considered improper for a younger person to initiate the more familiar way of calling someone by their first name. By now it has come to her attention that I will travel to the Cote d'Azure for Christmas, a fact which impresses her, and I am introduced to all the people I will be working with on a regular basis. This is the building mainly devoted to reinsurance, the big and very profitable risks and sets itself apart from the regular insurance business. I feel very lucky to work in such a wonderful office in close proximity of all Board Members who actually run the different company divisions. Every Monday morning their desks are decked out with huge bouquets of flowers, delivered by one of Cologne's premier florists, and everything is virtually perfect. The mail is delivered by a uniformed doorman. We enjoy a special status working out of the executive building. My co-worker previously worked for the EEC in Brussels as a translator and comes from a family which owns a business selling spare-parts for expensive cars. Consequently in the German hierarchy I am again on a lower level. Will I ever outgrow my working class status? I am beginning to wonder!

While the work is not very difficult, the insurance business is rather "dry" but I enjoy it anyway. As negotiated I am able to take the time between Christmas and New Year's off, leaving on Boxing Day for the Cote d'Azure.

Roger is waiting for me at the train station as usual with open arms. We look forward to the New Year's celebration and the time we will be able to spend together. Meanwhile his friends have become my friends and I have been corresponding in English with his sister for a while. We are very much in love and, other than during the frequent extremely deep philosophical discussion we tend to have, we mostly spend time in each other's arms.

Our first love is like a fever which consumes us with great intensity and will not break. We are physically and intellectually incredibly attracted to each other but stop short of taking the final step, because we also remain very much dedicated to our future. After all, Roger has a long time yet to go in medical school.

However, keeping our hearts and passion in check is becoming increasingly difficult for both of us.

That particular New Year's Eve we spend driving through Monte Carlo and end up in a well-known Disco just outside of Nice, called "Les freres de la Cote" (the brothers of the coast). The Beatles have just come out with their latest hit "Lucy in the sky with diamonds" and we dance until the wee hours of the New Year. Antibes is very beautiful and serene during the winter months. The snow reaches down much farther during the winter and so the contrast between palm trees, flowers, the blue Mediterranean and the snow-capped mountains in the distance is nothing less than breathtakingly beautiful. I do not like using superlatives, but this is truly what it is like.

Naturally the exotic surroundings add to my feelings of being in love, happiness and freedom. Actually, I cannot think of a time I have ever been happier in my life and trust this union will eventually lead to a happy marriage. While he has told me many times that he loves me, by now we talk more frequently of spending eternity together and I promise to wait for him, no matter how long it takes. We do consider ourselves engaged and his parents are quite happy with their son's choice since I am not distracting him from his studies. On the contrary, I am a very positive influence on him. Especially his mother makes no secret of how much she likes me.

Even when she finds out by sheer coincidence that we spent the night together in a hotel in Antibes, there are no raised eye-brows or reproaches.

All too soon I find myself on the train back to Germany. It is difficult to leave but we have obtained permission from his parents to spend our vacation together during the coming summer. His father will let us use the car and we make plans to travel through Italy, stopping in Florence, Rome and finally driving back along the Adriatic Coast all the way from the very bottom of the "boot" that forms Italy. An exciting prospect! When I come home and tell my parents they are not very supportive, but by the time we will go I will have reached the age of 21 and there is nothing they can do to prevent me from going.

Back at work I mope around for quite a while. Cologne is terribly dull and dreary during the winter and there is little to bring me out of my funk.

The letters keep going back and forth as usual and I am glad my parents cannot understand French. They might not like what we write to each other.

My co-worker and her husband ask me to go out with them occasionally and try to "fix" me up with one of their friends but I have no interest in them.

My heart is spoken for.

It really irks me that in the office is has become my job to wash the coffee cups and that the phone we share is always on my co-worker's desk. We sit facing each other and I resent being put in an inferior position. I have been there too many times before and so once in a while the cups remain unwashed.

There is no coffee break on those days, she simply refuses to do them herself and, though there is just her and her husband living in an apartment, she has a maid to do her weekly cleaning. Her mother, also living in an apartment, likewise has a maid. Growing up the way I have that is so unthinkable to me that one day, when the maid does not show up and my co-worker collapses into a heap of tears calling Mommie in order to borrow her maid, I am unable to show much sympathy for her plight. We come from different "classes" and there is a gulf which I will never be allowed to cross. Resentfully I accept my fate but also make a pledge to myself not to participate in this class nonsense in the future. Although being engaged to a medical student and hopefully eventually becoming his wife will elevate my status, I will not change in that respect. I will treat every person equally well.

On occasion a meeting requires my interpreting skills. One such event takes place when I am asked to interpret for the President of Renault, an American, who is coming to Cologne in order to negotiate a major reinsurance project.

The business negotiation ends with a formal luncheon and naturally I am asked join. When the distinguished customer notices that due to my interpreting the conversation I do not get a chance to eat, he asks me to convey to the other members that he would prefer a few minutes of silence, so I can eat myself.

He is a very nice gentleman, considerate and kind.

After the business meeting is over he has some time prior to catching his train back to Paris. In a very proper fashion he inquires if I could show him my hometown since this is his first visit to Cologne. Returning to my office I call my superior and ask him for permission to act as a guide to this important customer. To my great surprise he is very straightforward: "Is he an old lecherous man? I am responsible for you young Lady!" "No," I answer, "he is very kind and polite, there has not been any indication of improper intentions." "Very well then, go ahead," he says," but be careful; if he does anything inappropriate you have my permission to leave him immediately wherever you happen to find yourself and take a taxi back to the office at my expense. Don't give the business aspect another thought, just take care of yourself." That day I gain a new respect for my boss. He is the head of all the foreign offices of this large company and yet he is concerned for my wellbeing. Though he usually treats me in a rather distant fashion, this shows me another kinder side of his personality. With his blessings I become the tour guide for the President of Renault, starting out with the Cathedral of course and then other points of historical and cultural interest. He is very appreciative. We have the traditional "Kaffee und Kuchen" (coffee and cake) in the late afternoon and then we take a taxi to the train station where I see to it that he gets to the correct platform. Then I wait with him until his train departs for Paris. What a pleasant day this was, but I am also totally exhausted.

Interpreting is very stressful and these were high-level negotiations involving very large premium amounts. When I get home I fall into bed without even eating supper.

Now that I am gainfully employed I pay my parents 150DM each month, I have a savings account and I also spend a fair amount of money on nice clothing.

Within no time at all I have a wonderful assortment of business clothes, making my co-worker and me stand out as the best dressed young women in the entire building. We have lunch together every day in the cafeteria and don't go unnoticed.

"Here comes the Translation Department," we hear quite often. Young men from different departments stop by and linger for conversation and whenever visitors, such as the heads of foreign offices walk by the glass doors to the hallway, I can see them checking us out. In particular the head of the Milan office. I swear if he could turn his neck around any further he would look like an owl. He is a very handsome man, Italian Aristocracy and well known for his philandering.

I like to tease him by looking back straight into those roving fiery eyes, which I am sure, are in the process of undressing me every time he passes.

The workload is steadily increasing and eventually we have a meeting with our superior, asking him for a dictating machine, so we can dictate translations from English or French into German and have them typed by the typing pool. We receive what we ask for and this makes our life much easier since now we only have to type the documents which are to be translated into the foreign language.

Sometimes we get called to translate an article from a foreign business magazine by one of the Board Members.

There is one of them in particular we have to watch out for. Since my co-worker is married he shows restraint, but since I am single and younger I find out in time that I have to be on my guard. On one occasion he has his secretary call me to translate an article from the British Economist for him regarding insurance matters. Once I am done he corners me and tries to kiss me.

Sexual harassment not being an issue of concern for a man back then, I am on my own here, and who is going to take the word of a translator/interpreter over the word of a senior Member of the Board? Nevertheless, I slap his cheek and by the time I get home I have a rash near my mouth where his lips touched me. He could be my grandfather for God's sake! I am disgusted and upset but when my mother asks me about the rash I make up a story that I got bitten by some insect. The rash stays for a good week and I promise myself that, if in the future he has his secretary call me to work for him, I will demand his secretary stay in the room.

During the first year of work my home life is of little concern to me. I am so busy and spend very little time there. The acrimonious atmosphere continues unabated, but as long as they leave me out of their struggles I detach as much as I can. My mother is bored at home and when she calls me at the office I am often busy and short-tempered, something I will regret in later years. But I resent her trying to live through me vicariously instead of living her own life. I wish she would do something with herself other than clean the house and cook, now that we are all grown up. But she feels she has worked enough, not realizing that a person needs a challenge, a hobby or an occupation. I have no right to judge my mother, but I do realize now that she is deeply unhappy, depressed and is looking for happiness outside herself where it cannot be found. Later on I will regret not having shown more compassion for her plight. I am too young to understand the trauma she has dealt with and that has left her, as well as my father, deeply scarred for life.

All I want is to be left alone and live my life without their interference; without being drawn into the continuous dissonance which reigns my life at home. The Tumbleweed wants to be left alone and roam, but a lot of events have to take place which are extremely painful and will push me to the very edge of tolerance and acceptance of what I am emotionally able to endure.

On my 21st birthday I throw a big party at my home, inviting all my friends and asking them not to bring any gifts, just roses because they are my favorite. The living room is decked out with a large buffet and plenty of Champagne, after all, a girl does not turn 21 every day. The room also ends up full of roses and everyone enjoys themselves. Even my parents get dressed up for the occasion and seem to be in good spirits. Now I am legally independent and responsible for myself. Of course Roger calls that night to wish me a happy birthday! While mine is in June, he will turn 21 in August.

I am looking forward to our journey through Italy, our first vacation alone, but while we had planned to leave the first week in July, I receive a phone call informing me that he has to repeat one exam which he failed. Thus we cannot leave until the second week in July. When the day for my departure arrives I am dizzy with happiness. Travelling together will be an adventure and our love will finally move on to the next stage. I am well prepared.

A Broken Heart

This time the 16 hour train ride seems endless. With great anticipation and a pounding happy heart I finally arrive, ready to throw myself into the open arms that await me. However, as soon as I step off the train my heart feels a stabbing pain. I am very perceptive and the instant we look at each other and he gives me a brotherly kiss on the cheek, I know for sure that something has changed. Something is terribly wrong! During the drive to his parent's place he is totally quiet and distant. I feel myself entering a strange twilight zone. Roger drops me off at his home where I will share his sister's room until we leave, excuses himself with the explanation that he has to run some errands and disappears for several hours. Like usual, I am well received by his parents and his sister but deep down in the pit of my stomach I know that things have changed. I do not understand! Upon Roger's return we take a ride to the beach in Alassio.

On the way there he proceeds to tell me that during the week of the postponed vacation, after passing his exam, he met a young French girl from Paris and that he has been seeing her ever since. Apparently the previous evening they had gotten into an accident with his father's car. I am devastated!

The closeness we had for years is no longer there. He does not touch me and avoids my questioning eyes. For this trip I had purchased a special bikini, a tiny one in bright turquoise which fits me like a glove and there are many young men at the beach today looking at me. However, the young man whom I am madly in love with, the only person who matters to me does not seem to notice. He comments

199

that I seem to have put on some weight. Birth control pills will do that to you! His mother had asked me to take proper precautions.

She is a modern woman with good sense and I respect her greatly. That sunny afternoon I don't even see the beauty around me. The mountains, the colorful flowers, palm trees and the blue ocean, all of it has lost the radiance it used to have. My mind is reeling while he tells me that he happened to meet this sixteen year old Parisian girl at the beach and that, while he had dropped me off at his parents' house, went back there to spend some time with her and say good-bye.

I actually feel sick to my stomach. How could everything change within one lousy week. How could he love me and than meet a mere child who comes between us, our plans for the future, our lives? I am floundering like a fish out of water and have a hard time holding it together. I do not want to fall apart right there on that crowded beach. The hurt is almost unbearable, I am wounded to my very core fully realizing now that things will never be the same between us.

We leave early the next day. His mother is waving to us, wishing us a safe journey and a wonderful vacation. The miles tick by without a word being spoken. What is there to say? Finally we reach the Strada del Sol, the main highway leading to Florence. We stop for lunch somewhere but I cannot eat a bite. I don't notice anything on the trip. The pain I feel pierces my heart like a knife and leaves me in a numb, surreal state of mind.

Eventually we reach Florence and find a hotel where we sign in as Mr. and Mrs.. Florence is full of young couples on their honeymoon. When it is time for dinner I find myself sitting in the beautiful dining room overlooking the entire town, it's sweet aroma entering through the open windows and we are surrounded by happy couples holding hands. I make it half-way through the meal. Then I get up, leave the dining room in a hurry and return to our room where I throw myself on the bed and finally allow myself to fall apart. He follows accusing me of making a scene, but I really don't care at this point if the entire town of Florence hears me crying.

That night is one of the most memorable nights of my life. I am 21 years old and if, for the first time, I am going to give myself to someone, at least let it be a person I love. Although I know in my heart that the relationship is over I allow him to love me. But love is absent that night and the experience less than enjoyable, as a matter of fact it is extremely painful and I end up in a physician's office. Roger was forced to call him and he came, especially for me, having to return from his weekend home in the Tuscan countryside. The doctor is a handsome fifty-something Patrician looking man who examines me, takes care of my injury and talks to me for quite a while in English, since that is the only language we have in common. I shall never forget his kind words.

He tells me that he can heal my body but that it will take a long time and another love for my heart to heal. When Roger pays the bill I notice that the doctor is not that kind to him, but not speaking Italian I cannot understand what he is saying. All I can sense is that he feels sorry for me and blames Roger for my unfortunate experience. His face is stern while he talks to him and we leave the office quietly.

So we are forced by circumstances to stay for another few days allowing me to heal. We do visit the sites of Florence and once, while waiting in front of the Uffizi alone, a young American man approaches me. He asks me if I would like to share a cup of coffee with him in one of the sidewalk cafes when Roger returns and gets extremely angry. I guess this is the Italian possessive part of him. I am told in no uncertain terns that while with him, I have no right to talk to anyone else.

If I were not hurting as badly as I am I would have laughed, because his behavior makes no sense to me at all. Another day we take a ride into the charming Tuscan countryside. The rolling gentle hills are dotted here and there by small villages with ancient houses but all the beauty is dulled by my pain. Roger likewise knows it is over, but strangely enough he wants to continue our journey, at least to Rome.

I, on the contrary, insist on returning to his parent's home from where I will leave and spend the rest of my vacation by myself. It hurts too much being near him, and so we return to his parents' great surprise. When they find out what happened and I will not come out of my room to join them in their meals because I am so devastated that I feel ill, his mother gets very upset. She comes, sits by my bedside and talks to me. But her words are of little solace, I feel betrayed and know that things will never be the same. "Stay please," she says, "he will come to his senses," but she cannot not understand that it does not matter any longer. The damage to the relationship is done and I just have to get away. The next day I leave for a destination further down the Cote d'Azure ending up in Toulon. When I see Roger's mother for the last time before he takes me to the train station she actually yells at him, saying he is an imbecile for letting a girl like me go. Once again she begs me to stay but I have made up my mind. With my heart in shreds I leave in a dream-like state of confusion. The rest of my vacation is spent in a fog. I force myself to go out on dates, but my heart is broken and it will take a long, long time to mend. Never in my life, not even when I was little, have I felt such pain. I am too young to know that everything happens for a good reason; that bad experiences can lead to good outcomes and subsequent changes in our lives we could never have anticipated in our wildest dreams.

When I return home in a morose state I tell my parents who actually seem to be relieved. They never were quite happy with my choice, being engaged to a foreigner they could hardly understand. I return to work and throw myself into the Cologne nightlife full force in order to forget, but I do not have a good time.

That fall I decide to correct something that has been bothering me for a very long time. My smile, that is the alignment of my front teeth, still leaves a lot to be improved upon. Since I am an interpreter and as such spend a lot of time in public with customers, my appearance is important and the insurance company agrees to foot the bill for having my entire front teeth capped. After speaking to a reputable dentist in my area who comes highly recommended, I leave one Saturday morning to undergo the procedure.

It takes six hours to grind down the teeth, remove the cap I got for my birthday and naturally a novocaine injection is administered every twenty minutes.

Half way through the grinding process even the dentist starts to get tired.

It seems to me that I have been sitting in the dentist's chair for months.

On my 20 minute walk home, I feel strange and rather weak. While there are temporary caps hiding the stumps of my teeth, by the time I arrive home and look into the mirror my gums have turned black, absolutely black from the trauma of the continuous grinding. Much like a bruise they stay black for at least a week. As a matter of fact, I am in such pain, that I am confined to bed for three days. Then I return to work with my temporary caps and anxiously wait for the real ones to be finished. Within two weeks my smile for once is unencumbered and my "pearly whites" are much admired in the office. Some of my co-workers knew about my ordeal but it was well worth it.

No longer will I hear: "you would be a really pretty girl, were it not for your teeth." No, that is now something else in the past I can forget and look forward to a social life where I do not have to feel awkward smiling or laughing. Some people would not have cared, but being called "Vampire" all through my school years, as well as hearing the above statement frequently, made me take the pain, endure it and come out of the experience with something positive to show for.

From now on that will be my philosophy, no pain no gain. No matter what the circumstances, it is not what happens to us that matters but how we deal with it!

It is a good philosophy but easier said than done. At times the struggle to turn something negative into a positive direction takes all the strength I have.

My last year in Germany

Eva meanwhile has met the man of her life. After taking a long time to forget her first love in Spain, she is now dating a young man from Geneva, Switzerland, who will end up becoming her husband. Susanne is dating someone who is very possessive and manipulative. She has a hard time saying "no" and making up her mind. I don't think she really loves him.

That Christmas I receive a letter from Roger telling me that he was on his way to see me, wishing to ask for my forgiveness. He got as far as Switzerland and lost his courage. While I don't doubt that indeed, he is sorry, I also know that where he lives every year the beaches attract pretty young girls from the North and, that what I experienced, would repeat itself in the future. So in my return letter I forgive him but leave no doubt that the relationship is over and cannot be repaired. I wish him well and even though it pains me greatly, I know my decision is the right one.

In future years, once he has become a physician, he will visit my parents long after I have left, in order to find out how I am doing and to alleviate his guilty conscience. But it is far too late. He does not marry until he is in his mid-30s and even announces the birth of his first child to my parents.

Why, other than to convey this news to me, will always be a mystery. I continue dating and go through the motions pretending to have a good time.

However, much like grief over the death of a loved one, a broken heart takes time to heal. In my case it takes years until I allow myself to love again.

My work at the Insurance Company is much appreciated. The head of the department is happy with my performance; I even get daring and accept a date with the sexy head of the Milan office, which turns out to be a big disappointment. He is all looks with not much else to offer, plus he turns out to be married and I do not believe in dating married men. So this is the first and last time I accept an invitation for dinner, since his roving hands are not appreciated either.

That year I have no plans for New Year's Eve and so my mother wants to take a trip to Innsbruck asking me to accompany her. My father has to work the night shift and does not seem to mind. Mama has free railroad passes left and I decide to go along. The ride through the wintry Alps is therapeutic. The snow glistens like diamonds in the sun and at least this is a way to get my mind off my broken heart. Mama and I stay at an old-fashioned hotel in the center of town and take the bus every day as well as cable cars to various points of interest. From there we usually hike on the snowy paths.

Basically we have a good time together. She is careful not to mention Roger and we attend the New Year's Eve party at the hotel. It seems that everyone but me has a date for the evening, and so I feel totally out of place. After dinner we decide to retreat to our room way before midnight. We go to bed and read while Innsbruck is ringing in the New Year. At the time I don't know that this will be the last New Year's Eve I spend in Europe.

The fresh mountain air does both of us good, though we don't really communicate a lot. I have a hard time talking to my mother about feelings. She always seems to direct the conversation back to her own plight and wrong choice in men, my father, and so we mostly talk about superficialities.

Also there is such a gulf between us. While she has much more life experience, I have a better education and a totally different view of life in general. As far as she is concerned, a woman belongs in the home with children, whose ultimate duty it is to make their mother happy. I, on the other hand, enjoy my work and believe in creating my own happiness.

Upon our return home events escalate yet again. My mother has been extremely belligerent towards my father and he has started seeing another woman, leaving the house on Sundays when he is off dressed in his best clothes with a big smile on his face. Needless to say my mother is perplexed and withdraws, most likely wondering what is happening. Her tirades have finally succeeded in driving my father to the point where he has chosen to look elsewhere. I can sense what is coming and decide that, considering the ending of my own first love affair, as well as what I will be facing at home, the time for me to leave has come. Gradually I begin to scan the employment pages concentrating on job offers abroad. I am sick and tired of the constant rain in the Rhineland, the low clouds, the moody people who surround me and the guilt that clings to me like glue. Finally I am sick and tired of living in GERMANY! I feel that I will suffocate if I do not get out of the confines of this strangling environment soon. A few months later I find an interesting job offer by an American Company in Brussels, send them my resume and receive a call back, asking me to come in for an interview. This happens to be around Easter and I am off between Good Friday and Easter Monday.

Good Friday I leave by train from the main train station in Cologne for Brussels, where I take a taxi which brings me to the location of the American Company. While Brussels is a lovely city, the position is with an American

Chemical Company on the outskirts of Brussels. My heart sinks when I enter the offices, because by now I have become accustomed to my plush office in Cologne with the Insurance Company. However, I can always find an apartment in the charming center of Brussels. The interview goes very well. The first day I am back at work after Easter I receive a call from the person I interviewed with.

They are offering me the position at a salary beyond my wildest dreams. I tell them that I have to think about it for a couple of days, but basically I am willing to make the move.

Unbeknownst to me, a co-worker in the adjoining office, a young man who for some reason does not care for me nor I for him, since he is your typical lawyer from a "superior family" with great aspirations, has overheard my conversation and decides to take the information straight to my boss.

However, as is the case quite often, evil intentions turn around and lead to something positive, because my boss asks me to come to his office, to sit down and confronts me with the news he has heard regarding my desire to leave the company. I tell him that indeed, I have an excellent offer in Brussels from an American firm, and he asks me for the reason I wish to leave.

At this point I break out into tears. All I have held back pours out of me in front of this distinguished man, who thoughtfully reaches for his starched white handkerchief handing it across the desk. I tell him about my broken engagement, my horrible circumstances at home and he looks at me compassionately saying: "well, we just have to get you out of this situation."

"Did you ever think of transferring within the company?" I didn't. I had not even considered that. He suggests that since he is the head of all the foreign offices, I ought to give some serious thought to this avenue. "Right now," he says, "I could place you into our offices in Paris, Johannesburg or New York City." "Think about it and let me know your preference, because I am going on my annual visit of all the foreign offices within the next few weeks." I am dumbfounded, thank him profusely for his compassion as well as the offer and promise to make a speedy decision. Over the coming weekend I make my choice. New York City is it! I inform the Company in Brussels that I have had a better offer and have committed myself. My boss is happy, wondering if I can start in New York on October 1st. At this time the process to obtain a visa is rather lengthy. I have to apply for a Treaty Trader Visa and commit myself to stay for a time span of two years. The company will pay for my flight and my first week's expenses, after which I will be on my own, working in the Steuben Glass building, on the 18th floor right on 5th Avenue, corner of 56th and 57th Street, a very desirable neighborhood uptown near Central Park and the Plaza Hotel. We agree on a salary and everything seems to fall into place. It sounds heavenly and exciting.

Finally I will be able to spread my wings and become a true Tumbleweed.

But it is only shortly after Easter and before leaving there is another vacation planned with an old high-school friend of mine to Marbella, Spain.

She went there on a vacation the previous year and wanted to return, looking for someone to come along. I have never been to Spain and I have never flown in an airplane. We are scheduled to spend three weeks in Marbella in May/June and I really look forward to this trip.

At home my father has approached me on several occasions regarding his desire to divorce my mother, but since the house and everything else is in her name, he needs proof that living conditions are intolerable. Once again I am being drawn right square into the middle and I avoid touching this subject whenever possible. My mother has gotten more and more suspicious of my father's frequent absences but I do not tell her where he goes. I don't feel it is any of my business or responsibility. I cannot wait to get out and going to Spain for three weeks will surely help. With great anticipation I wait for May to arrive and the second week in May we leave from Duesseldorf Airport on a charter flight to Malaga, where a bus picks us up taking us along the Costa del Sol to our final destination in Marbella.

Adventures in Spain

I reach the airport in Duesseldorf with some trepidation having never flown before. My girl friend tells me it is wonderful, especially the take-off.

She say's it is like being in a car and going really fast, only faster than you can imagine until, all of a sudden, you are airborne. She is right, I love flying and am almost sorry once we land in Malaga. The coastline somewhat reminds me of Southern France or Northern Italy, my favorite combination of mountains and ocean. A bus takes us to our final destination, making a stop in Torremolinos, where some of the passengers from the same flight will spend their vacation. To me Torremolinos is horrible, huge high-rise hotels right at the ocean front. How could they spoil such a beautiful coastline? I am relieved when we reach Marbella because while there are some larger hotels, the town is still intact with its Plaza Major, the meeting place for the locals, surrounded by charming stores and restaurants. We stay in a medium-sized hotel, our accommodations consisting of a large living room, bedroom, a small kitchen and a full bath. However the very best part is the balcony overlooking the Mediterranean. Since Birgit has been there before and knows her way around, we unpack quickly and then go out exploring. The weather is gorgeous and the architecture in the old town charms me. I love to peek into the court-yards containing fountains, a profusion of flowers and native plants. The only thing I dislike about Spain are the constantly begging children, not leaving us alone, as well as the liberties young Spanish men take, pinching young foreign girls from the North who stand out quite distinctly. That has never happened to me before and for the remainder of the vacation it will be an annoyance I cannot get used to. In a way it makes me feel violated. When reprimanded, they simply laugh and don't pay any further attention other than joking amongst each other.

Marbella is located not too far from Gibraltar but we never get there, even though we had intended to do so. My girl friend falls in love with a young and very handsome Spaniard within the first few days and that limits our activities. I don't really mind. On occasion we go out on separate dates but I am still grieving and struggling with my loss. At the beach I meet a young man who physically is the spitting image of my former love. We go out on a date but he is nothing like him. He totally lacks Roger's depth and charm. Needless to say the first date is our last. My girlfriend's love interest has a brother and sometimes we double date, but there is absolutely no chemistry between us. Nevertheless, knowing and going out with natives from the area leads to some unforgettable experiences which make our vacation infinitely more enjoyable. One day they take us by car into the mountainous hinterland promising us a very special treat. We drive up to a certain point where we have to leave the car behind, get on donkeys which carry us further up the steep mountainside, to an ancient village called Ojen. Like a swallow's nest it is attached to the steep mountain and women are in the process of washing their laundry in the stream below. We are definitely not a sight the local inhabitants are used to and so we walk through the village with all eyes upon us and hoards of children in tow. The houses are all stark white, a beautiful contrast to the green mountains and the dark blue sky with the Mediterranean shimmering in the distance. Some of the old women dressed in black are busy white-washing the houses which, from doing so for centuries, have no corners left. All edges are rounded and somehow remind me of artworks by Salvador Dali. We are asked inside some of the homes which have dirt floors and where chickens as well as other farm animals freely walk in and out.

We watch women baking bread and are invited to drink some tea which is delicious. With the little Spanish I know we converse plus the brothers act as interpreters. I did not know such medieval places still existed in Europe. Totally untouched by modern civilization's conveniences.

The other experience is likewise memorable and we would have missed out on it completely, had it not been for the Spanish brothers.

On another day they take us again into the mountains up from the coast, where a stream spilling down the rugged mountainside in a little gorge collects and forms a small pool, surrounded by blossoming azaleas.

The water is warm and crystal clear, inviting us to shed our clothes and in our underwear we enjoy the beauty of the surrounding mountains.

It is like sitting in a hot-tub, prior to the invention of hot tubs. All this is quite harmless and proper, we are simply four youngsters having fun.

Most of the days are spent at the beach, and although in May the water of the Mediterranean is still quite chilly, we have a good time. We do not have to worry about lunch since directly underneath the promenade, running along the beachfront, a group of restaurants offers the finest paella made to order which we wash down with copious amounts of Sangria. Afterwards we go back to our beach chairs and doze away the afternoon in the warm rays of the sun. Spain has some strange customs though. People do not eat dinner until very late at night. Often we have something to eat in our little apartment, then take a nap until about 10p.m. It seems most restaurants don't even open before then, and the normal time to go out for dinner is after 11p.m. One day we take the bus to explore Malaga and have lunch in a wonderful restaurant perched on a rock outcropping overlooking the Mediterranean. On our way there we are pinched yet again by young Spaniards who laugh at our expense. How very annoying! Why can't they keep their hands to themselves?

Malaga is a beautiful city and while I would have loved to visit Seville, time does not allow us to do so.

For my 22nd birthday my girl friend takes me to see a bullfight. It does not take long for me to decide that this is one "sport" I can never learn to enjoy. Once the Picadors have weakened the poor bull who is standing there helplessly stunned and hurt, I close my eyes for most of the rest of the event. My girl friend loves it, but I feel this is the most cruel sporting activity I have ever seen. The Torero is not very skilled in killing the bull and when the huge animal finally dies, the arena is so bloody that I cannot wait to leave. I do not want to spoil my girl friend's fun but I do not ever intend to see another bullfight. This is not a sport in my eyes, but instead the senseless slaughter of a scared animal. Frankly, I hated what I witnessed.

During the last week I have a close brush with death myself. Sometimes we don't realize how fragile life can be and how fortuitous our fortunes are.

While laying in the sunshine at the beach on a beach-towel and talking to a young Frenchman on my left, having my head turned in his direction, he suddenly pushes me with all his force out of the way of an oncoming beach umbrella swept up by the wind. It was headed for my bare midsection, spike first, and embeds itself firmly in the shinbone of the lady behind me. I am thoroughly shaken fully realizing that, had he not pushed me out of the way, I would have been impaled and could have died. As it is, the lady it hit is screaming in great pain until the ambulance arrives and takes her away. I am shaken by the experience and I thank the young man who saved me from harm. After that, from hereon, I am not comfortable with beach umbrellas anywhere. Little do I realize that over 30 years later I will have yet another serious encounter with a beach umbrella, a very close brush with disaster where I actually get hurt badly in the Caribbean.

My fear of beach umbrellas with spiked tips is well founded. The remainder of the vacation passes without any further incidence. My girl friend has seriously fallen in love with Hernandez and we spend the last night enjoying a bit too much Sangria. By the time we set out for the airport in Malaga I do not feel well at all. At the airport Birgit tells me that I look rather "green" and sickly which I am, but the proverbial "barf-bag" remains unused during the flight back to Duesseldorf.

I take a taxi home from Birgit's house since a bus picked us up in Duesseldorf and I arrive at home in great spirits. We had an enjoyable vacation and the transfer to New York will take place within the not too distant future. Life is looking up, finally! I feel like I am about to emerge from the other end of a long dark tunnel, about to break free.

The first night back I can sense increased tension at home. Since it is Sunday, a good friend of mine and I go to a local restaurant within walking distance of my home for dinner and to talk about my vacation adventures. I am in extremely high spirits. We are laughing and having a good time, when suddenly, outside of the restaurant window, I see the totally desperate face of my father. He is holding his bicycle in his shaking hands and his face is bleeding.

I rush outside to see what happened, assuming he might have been in an accident, but he is almost incoherent. In a great state of agitation he tells me that my mother found a letter intended for the woman he has been seeing, and confronted him when he came home from work outside the house in full view of the entire neighborhood. When he tried to remove the letter from her hands she scratched his face and actually kicked him fiercely.

Instantly my heart sinks to the bottom of my feet, it cannot possibly drop any lower. One minute I am sitting relatively carefree in a lovely restaurant, and next I am once again thrown into the abyss of my despair. My father, my friend and I set out on foot for the short walk home. Once again I hear:

"If it had not been for the WAR, none of this would have happened." The WAR! I am so damned tired hearing about the WAR, yet feeling its ugliness touching my life in so many ways. Whenever I travel the only thing that lightens my burden and the utter shame of being German is the fact that I happen to be a pretty young girl. But like an evil monster it continues to reach into the present and haunts me. Damn that bloody War, damn Hitler, damn all those stupid people who felt they were the "super-race." To me they were nothing but a bunch of hoodlums, fools who ruthlessly made their way to the top by eliminating most of Germany's intelligent people, either just doing away with them or forcing them to leave the Country, then intimidating the average population with their Blockwardens, threats and stupid promises of a Thousand Year Reich. What a joke! How could anybody have fallen for that nonsense. And all those damn cowards who, instead of fighting on the different fronts, took the easy way out, terrorizing and brutally killing millions of innocent Jewish people as well as those resisting Hitler's reign. What kind of courage does it take to point your rifle at unarmed people? What incredible insensitivity, and evil to march millions naked into gas chambers, place human remains, those of men, women and children into ovens to destroy the evidence. Where was the God I pray to when all this happened? Didn't anybody read "Mein Kampf," the ravings of an obviously unstable person? And where was the rest of the world, those who knew and did nothing? Where are they now? Why am I stamped guilty when I was not even born? And my parents and grandparents, at what point is the instinct for self-preservation, especially when young children are at stake, an acceptable reason for trying so survive? Both my father and mother spoke out, but they were young and both of them had to take into account the lives of their small children. And the ensuing nightmare of losing loved ones, losing everything and from the rubble having the strength left to rise up and to build new lives. Are all of us condemned to carry this burden resting so heavy on our shoulders to our graves? When is enough enough?

How often in the future will I have to listen about this abominable WAR, THE HOLOCAUST, THE MONSTROUS GERMAN SOUL? Was Stalin a Saint?

History is full of atrocities, yet we are not ever allowed to talk of our own pain and suffering! How strange. How very strange!

All these are thoughts going through my young mind while walking home. My father is babbling about how I have to help him see to it that he gets a divorce. I am not even listening but following my own train of thoughts.

When we arrive at home my mother is standing in the walkway to the house, a half-torn letter in her hand crying.

"I cannot see," she keeps saying, "I am going blind!" Being only able to see with one eye that is her ultimate fear, ever since she was little and, due to a tumor, lost her sight completely in her left eye. She also uses it as the ultimate tool of manipulation, that much I know. At a loss of what to do and totally humiliated by the spectacle that is taking place outside for all the neighbors to watch and hear, I stand between them trying to calm them down, when all of a sudden each of them literally grabs one of my arms, pulling me in opposite directions while imploring me do to something. This is my breaking point! Tears begin streaming down my face that was so happy and smiling just half an hour ago. While I stand there helplessly, I feel myself being pulled apart, body, mind and soul, all of it.

I think I will go insane if this nightmare does not stop. Finally my friend steps up to the plate. Usually a mild-mannered young man who attended College with me, he too has reached his limit. "Don't you see what you are doing to your daughter?" he yells at them. "You are destroying her. Act like adults and leave her out of your problems." He pulls me away from them forcefully and with a quivering voice orders me to go into the house, get my work clothes and some necessities for a couple of days, because he is taking me home with him. Like in a trance I do as told, all the while tears continue to stream down my face. We leave my perplexed parents to deal with their own problems without having me in the middle as peacemaker or scapegoat to blame their troubles on. Walking home to his house, by now it is almost midnight, I am literally shaking and sobbing uncontrollably. He, being the good friend he is, does not try to stop me. When his mother opens the door she takes one look at me and compassion fills her eyes. My good friend tells her: "Inge is sleeping in my room tonight. I shall make my bed on the sofa." There is no need to ask any question. His mother fully understands and just leads me up to the room I am going to stay in, then leaves me alone to compose myself. I am unable to sleep. The ugly scenes I witnessed keep repeating themselves in my mind. When I get up in the morning my eyes are almost shut from crying.

So I hide behind sunglasses all day, even though it is dreary and rainy outside.

I feel like I have been beaten. My entire body hurts and though my co-worker would like to hear about my vacation, by now she knows about my circumstances and leaves me be.

Later on that day my boss calls to ask if it is possible for me to leave for New York City by mid-August. I am needed there. Is it possible? This is the greatest blessing I could have been offered. The date is set for August 14th 1969. He himself calls the Consulate to speed up my visa and his secretary makes the airline reservation. It is mid-June, so this means I only have to get through two months and I will be free. I am able to accomplish that I tell myself. After 22 years, what are two months? The thought of leaving everything behind, my terrible childhood, my struggles at the University, the memory of Roger, but most of all my painful home-life and this wretched country I grew up in and have come to dislike intensely, holds me up like a life jacket in a turbulent ocean. Every life has its dark sides, but it seems to me that for someone as young as I am, I have had more than my fair share and the idea of starting fresh is exhilarating.

After a couple of days I return home. At first neither of my parents are talking. The silence is deafening. In my mind I am totally focussed on my departure for the United States, for New York City and a new beginning. I will make it work. In a way I feel sorry for my mother. She is suffering the very pain I am by now familiar with myself, but on the other hand I think of all the pain she caused herself in taking another wife's man deliberately, and I see the strange irony in what is taking place. Be careful what you do, it just might return to you like a boomerang. For years she has been the unforgiving one, filled with disappointment, anger and even hate, but now she finds herself on the other side. One day, while Mama is shopping, Papa takes me aside to talk to me. He wants a divorce and he wants me to testify against my own mother in court. When I tell him no, that he is putting me in a terrible and quite unacceptable position, he gets very angry. Until I leave for New York he does not speak to me again. What he is asking of me is wrong. Is he ultimately so weak that he needs me to do the dirty work for him? Why does he refuse to take responsibility for his own actions? How could he have been so brave during the war, decline the order to go to Bergen Belsen as a guard, and yet be so weak when it comes to dealing with my mother? Is that what rejected love can do to a person? Although I know Mama is scared of my leaving, she is talking to me and I almost get the sense she herself wishes she could start all over again. But she cannot. This is something she has to see through herself. I cannot help her nor do I want to. I am through being beaten up in the middle. I am through taking responsibility for their unhappiness, the War, the Holocaust, the entire horror and mess that started and ended before I was even born, yet follows me, heaps guilt on me and punishes me for something I had nothing to do with. The aftereffects are devastating for so many members of the immediate post-war generation and we are never even allowed to talk about it. Not even in our own country. Even here it is a forbidden subject, and when abroad I have to be extremely careful not to offend anyone's sensibilities. Am I personally responsible for Ann Frank's death? I do not think so!

I am a very sensitive person with a tender heart and it pains me to know that there are people in this world who hate me, want nothing to do with me just because of my nationality. That mind-set is so foreign to me, it is simply beyond my comprehension, because I treat each person as an individual. I am unable to just see a group or nationality of people and decide I do not like them. My family got hurt during the War, I am suffering from the aftereffects but I hope that in the United States, the melting-pot of nations, I will be accepted for the person I am. How very naïve of me! But I am hoping anyway. After all, I am only 22 years old.

While I am making lists of items I shall take with me, work keeps me busy and my co-workers are planning a big going-away party for me. I avoid being at home as much as possible, with my father's stoic silence and my mother's uneasy communication. I do think she is grateful though that I am not willing to take my father's side. I go out as much as possible during the remainder of my stay in Germany. One night when I return home quietly, apparently my parents have not heard me. While standing downstairs in the foyer I hear my mother crying while my father is berating her. He is uttering very hurtful words. By now I have had it. I storm upstairs, open their bedroom door and tell them that they both are equally mean and cruel towards each other. How can they ask of me to respect them? After I have said my piece ending with the statement that I cannot wait to leave, I slam the door behind me and there is deathly quiet. It felt good to say what I did. I go to bed and sleep soundly. Why should I care any longer, I will be gone soon.

The good-bye party given at my co-worker's apartment turns out to be great fun.

Everybody comes, even my favorite professor from the University. It lasts until well into the night and the next week goes by in a blur of activity. My oldest sister and her three children have come from Bavaria where she now lives to spend the summer, and that takes a lot of the attention off me. Finally the day arrives for my departure and my parents, my oldest sister, her children, my co-worker and my good friend who rescued me that terrible night, accompany me to the airport. The last half hour is spent talking about the plane, a Boeing 707, then the largest plane in the skies, and my new life in New York. Some last minute snapshots are taken, I say my good-byes and for the first time my father speaks to me. I see tears in his eyes. We are both hurting but I try to smile and tell him: "I'll see you in two years." Everyone is under the impression that after my contract is fulfilled I will return. But I know better. Yes, I will return for an occasional visit, but I will never live here again. Never, so help me God.

Entering the boarding area I am not nervous or anxious in the least. Ahead of me I see the shining Boeing 707 airplane that will take me to a new world and I step aboard confidently. My seat is near the window on the other side, so I cannot see me relatives and friends until the plane starts to taxi down the runway and I watch them getting smaller and smaller, less and less significant in my life. Once we are airborne the gentleman sitting next to me asks where I am going. I tell him that I am being transferred by my company for two years to New York City. He is a former German, a man in his fifties who left Germany right after the war and settled in Wisconsin.

"You will like New York," he tells me, "I don't think you will go back to live in Germany." He looks at me and smiles. "American men are very attractive you know!"

There is a twinkle in his eyes. I like him! He says he could never go back to live in Germany again, he loves living in the United States.

The flight is uneventful and smooth. At one point, I am about mid-way across the Atlantic, I sit back, close my eyes and ask myself: "what on earth are you doing? You are going to a place where you do not know a soul." But the moment is brief. I have no regrets and a few hours later we descend over Long Island to land at Kennedy Airport in the late afternoon. While the plane is taxiing to the gate I am looking outside. I don't know what I had expected, but I see the same grass and weeds growing along the runway as at home, however when I step out of the plane and walk down the steps I take a deep breath and look up at the sky. The smell is different, the sky is higher and the feeling of absolute freedom envelopes me like a magic cloak.

At last, the Tumbleweed is free to tumble, stay for awhile and then let go again to follow the dreams unencumbered and to embark fully on the adventure that is life.

For now I am home, finally I have come home!

photo by: Roland Perreault

COMING TO TERMS

Today is my 54th birthday and I have asked my husband of 30 years to spend the day in Manhattan. I want to visit some of our most favorite places, eat at our favorite restaurant in Chinatown and take a ride on the Staten Island Ferry as we did so many years ago, just about two months after I landed in New York. He told me then, on the same ferry, that he would give me a reason to stay. He surely has. Compressing the past 32 years there is our courtship and marriage, transfer to Chicago and a five year stay there, working as a translator for one of Chicago's largest Patent Law Firms, the birth of my oldest son, my mother-in-law's untimely death -only 6 weeks between the birth of my son and his grandmother's death. They would have loved each other very much.

The subsequent move back to the East Coast, New Jersey to be specific, followed by the purchase of our first home. Next the birth of our second son, full-time motherhood with all that entails, the building of our dream house on a large and serenely beautiful piece of property, designed and built by us for the most part.

Then feeling the itch to do something again, besides being wife and mother, once my youngest son was about three years old. Starting a small building company, applying for my first line of credit in the only business suit I still owned after having lived in blue jeans for years when the children were small. With business plan in hand convincing the banker that my idea was viable. Walking out with shaking knees and a credit line much larger than expected, as well as making a profit on my first house, something the banker had not anticipated. My husband joining me in the business years later, all the ups and downs inherent in the industry and the economy in general. The entire spectrum from the highest high to the lowest low and during the entire time this wretched internal struggle with my past.

Ultimately, after having been misdiagnosed my entire life, having to face the fact that I suffer severely from Panic Anxiety Disorder as well as Depression, both the result of a genetic defect affecting the brain chemistry apparently inherited from my mother's side and made worse by my less than perfect childhood.

Coming to accept myself for who I was and who I have become during the enormous struggle within, while dealing with the ups and downs of life.

Being able to do both, the stay-at-home Mom and pursuing a home-based business. Guiding my sons through elementary school, the middle years, high school and then finally College. The marriage of my oldest son and struggling with the feelings of loss and separation. Watching the people whom I love struggle, right now my youngest son who does not know where his path will take him. But then do any of us know where our destiny will lead us? Maybe that is a good thing!

My husband and I in a new phase of our thirty year union struggle ourselves with the new paths and opportunities before us, while the fabric of the tapestry that is life unfolds right before our eyes and slowly the path becomes clearer.

My father has been dead for 6 years now. He died from a heart attack while I was returning from a visit to Germany, (in the later years I went by myself; it was easier for everyone) and I remember well both of us knowing that when saying our last good-bye, it would be just that, the last time we would see each other. By then he had visited us in the United States many times together with my mother. The marriage lasted till the very end, in spite of all the fights and grudges and the ugliness inherent in any dysfunctional relationship. My mother survived cancer at the age of 70 and has been ailing ever since. She has been living in an Assisted Care Facility where I last visited her when the house needed to be sold. It pained me not to see one photograph of my father or one of his paintings anywhere, and I could not bring myself to go back to the house for one last time. It was an empty shell. Built by my father's hands and now devoid of any of their cherished possessions I could not face looking at it. A lot of pain is connected with the memories, but I did love the garden and would rather remember everything as it once was. The only thing remaining today is the old horseshoe my friend saved, painted silver by my father and which once hung over the entrance doors of the shack as well as the new house for as long as I can remember.

While there I went to see my father's grave, distraught by the condition it was in. Quite apparently nobody had visited it in a long time. I know my mother did not once after the funeral, and so I found it overgrown with weeds and lacking a proper headstone. I stood there silently lost in my memories and grief, then went to work removing weeds and digging in the soil with tears in my eyes. My husband was with me but gave me space to do what I felt was necessary. Then we went to purchase flowers. A bleeding heart which was his mother's favorite, and some I knew he would have liked and needed little care, since there would not be anybody there in the future to care for them. I also ordered a proper headstone with his name and dates of his birth and death, as well as a surround that likewise would not require any care or upkeep. I doubt I ever will visit his grave again. Papa lives in my heart and what a better place is there to rest, than close to the ones we love.

His spirit and the good values he instilled in me are very much alive.

My mother went blind last year, is 89 years old and very infirm by now.

On Mother's Day I spoke to her and thanked her for giving me LIFE. Her once beautiful body is disintegrating rapidly and I call her twice a week now. I do not think she wants me to see her like this and frankly, I am afraid to go back. Mama does not want to live any more; yet she does not want to die either. She is scared, just like my once big, strong father was scared when I last took him to his physician and held his big hand in mine.

Will I be? My father knew, intuitively, that the end was near. To this very day I believe that he "postponed" his heart attack until I had left German soil, but I was fully aware that the end was imminent.

Yes, there had been lots of visits back and forth over the past 32 years, especially when the children were younger. Sometimes they were good and other times terribly upsetting. It took us as a very long time to come to terms and like one another. But in the end we did and that is the important part. I remember not telling my father for nine years that I had become a United States citizen and dropped my German citizenship like an uncomfortable garment,

burning it in my mind. Then, to my great surprise, long after he knew, had struggled with and finally accepted my decision, he told me on his last visit to the States: "If I had to do it all over again, I would have left Germany right after the war and done the same you did. You made a good life for yourself."

I don't think I ever told him just how much that meant to me and how some of the heavy shackles I have carried around with me dropped off that very moment. Like the

229

little girl who was praised for learning how to ride a bicycle, that compliment was so important for my spirit. I hope he knew without my saying so. Like me, he felt the sky was higher here and opportunity plentiful, in exchange for loss of a certain security. But then life always extracts a toll for taking a risk. For some people risk-taking is very difficult, and I often wonder just why I am such a risk taker. Maybe because I never felt I had that much to lose.

I love my parents and have long ago forgiven them for what was done to me unintentionally. They simply did not know any better and did the best they could. There is not much more we can ask of our parents, and I hope that someday my sons will come to the same conclusion. We have a much different relationship. They had a rather smooth childhood, but I am sure there are things I did wrong or buttons that get pushed, whether intentionally or not, that I will ask their forgiveness for; like they will ask for mine, and we shall do just that. Forgive one another the fact that we are not perfect, that we are just trying to get through this life the best we can with the tools that were handed down to us and which, at times, are not adequate to do the job of living right. That's where acceptance comes in.

Mama's character was formed by the hardships she experienced, the loss of sight in one eye when she was only four years old, having to take over my grandmother's household duties while she was sickly when my mother was young, and at an age when she could have learned a profession. The terrible war experience as a single mother, losing her beloved first husband at the age of only 28. Frankly, I do not think I could have managed as well as she did.

While I have never heard the words "forgive me," I know she has forgiven me my youthful follies and I am likewise eternally grateful to her for NOT teaching me how to cook when my father thought it was time to do so . She knew that I would have to for the rest of my life and thus allowed me to travel freely and enjoy my youth, not realizing that so often it was an escape for me. Mama was an outstanding cook, and I am proud to say that I am the only one of her three daughters who can cook a delicious Sauerbraten the way she did. The recipe will be handed down to my sons and their wives because that is one of her legacies, precious to all of us. She was and is next to my own Oma the best grand-and great-grandmother I have ever known.

Her "little" ones were and are the apple of her eye and she treated them all equally, never scolding any of them. She loved them and indulged them just as much as my father did. My own sons still talk about his "Ernie laughter" and the many hilarious pranks he involved them in. Both of my parents were fantastic grandparents. It is unfortunate that my mother never realized that she too had choices. She had a lot to offer to this world but the disease she passed down to me and to her other children was at the time not recognized or even known about. What a pity and now, that she is old and feeble she feels useless, not knowing that until her hour comes to leave this earth, there are still things she could contribute. I do love her dearly, she taught me what not to do simply by the mistakes she made, unknowingly passing on valuable lessons which have served me well.

My half-sisters on my mother's side are still part of my life, though I have not seen my oldest sister in 14 years. She is not well, mentally as well as physically. A damaged spirit

231

resulting from defective genes, the war and a very unhappy and unhealthy marriage. The last time I saw her my children, parents and I were visiting her oldest daughter, my niece, closer in age to me than my own sister. I hardly recognized her and she would slip in and out of her disease. I could see it in her eyes and, I am ashamed to admit, in a way it frightened me. The morning we left and waited on the platform of the train station she arrived riding her bicycle just in time to say good-bye.

There, on that platform, I met my oldest sister again, the way I remembered her when I was little and I don't think I ever loved her more than at that very moment. She must have ridden her bicycle for miles to reach us just in time and was so very happy she succeeded. Both of us had tears in our eyes and held each other tight. The bond was there and my compassion for her overwhelmed me. She did not deserve this. She never even had a childhood. After all, she was 12 years old when the war ended.

Nobody should experience what she did. It should not come as a surprise to anybody that she was scarred for life much more severely than I was.

Deep down she is a very generous, loving person and not to blame for her condition. But I could see that while she had given her best years to her daughters, they were unable to show her the respect she deserves, nor the empathy trying to understand the causes for her behavior. They struggled with it just like I did regarding my own mother and they were born into a different world. Unless you have walked in our shoes, you will simply not understand how hard it was for us, especially for her since she was thrown into the turmoil of war at such a tender age.

The nightmares she personally experienced and the anguish scarred her deeply. I will always love her, even if we never see each other again. At present we exchange Christmas cards and wish each other well, but I intend to try and resume a regular correspondence, as long as her letters are not too disturbing.

Sometimes, when I call my mother, I get to talk to my other half-sister who lives close to the nursing home, on my dime of course. Other than when my father died she has not called me but once in 32 years. We exchange pleasantries and life experience. She still plays the role of the older sister, always knowing better, being sicker, having a more difficult life than I do.

It is my guess that like my mother, she never realized either that she had options and I let her win in this unhealthy game of "one-downmanship," because unless she reads this book, she has no knowledge of the person I have become. Not once has she mentioned my published articles in magazines and newspapers, although I used to send my mother copies before she lost her eyesight. However, to my utmost surprise, I found a small package in the mail last Christmas, containing a little book of poems written in the native Cologne dialect. Reading it I found out why it was sent to me.

It contained a poem written by my sister. I never expected sibling rivalry from a woman past 60, but that is why I received my first Christmas gift from her in years. Usually I do not even receive a Christmas card, and if I do, is arrives long after the holidays have passed. Somehow this gift though told me of the burdens from the past she carries, and so I made it a point to heap great praise on her. However, our once strong bond was severed long ago, and once my mother dies we too shall exchange Christmas cards until the end and that will be alright.

The other half-siblings, the two daughters and one son from my father's first marriage are no longer a part of my life. They would never have been, had it not for a period of correspondence with the youngest one, who prior to the reunification of Germany was constantly in need of one thing or another, which I would dutifully provide. And then the meeting with my oldest half-sister, whose acquaintance I was unfortunate enough to make once, just prior to my father's death. I did not like her, instinctively and for good reason, as I was to find out later. Once employed by the Communist Government in what was then East Germany with extensive travel privileges, meaning that she must have been a trusted member and then, when the wall fell, she immediately found a nice position for herself and her spouse in the CDU, nicely moving up the ranks.

I have never seen my half-brother. His world collapsed along with the wall and communism, since that is what he taught as a professor at a prestigious East German University. Him I felt empathy for. His actions spoke of character to me, even if he misplaced his loyalty in giving it to a system that had nurtured him all through his life. I believe I would have liked to have known him but it is too late now. Two years after my father's death, one day a Sheriff knocked at my door and served me with a summons, a lawsuit, accusing me of absconding with their alleged share of my father's inheritance (I never received any). I was stunned and, after consulting with my lawyer, I was advised to simply stay out of Germany.

Even if, against all odds, they would have won the lawsuit, they would have had to enforce it here in the United States, hiring American attorneys at a tremendous expense to them. In the end they walked away with less money than they must have spent, for Mama had been clever and everything was in her name, other than some funds left in a bank account for Papa's burial. By then, intentionally, I did not make it easy for them either nor did I want to! I was tired of being the innocent victim once again and so they must have spent a fortune for the translation of a huge stack of legal documents which had to be translated by an expensive Court Certified Translator, since having been a United States Citizen for such a long time, I claimed not to understand the German legal lingo any longer. I do not care about them any more, nor do I ever wish to hear from them again. I have forgiven them in my heart, for they too had a difficult life. But mostly I had to forgive them for my own well being and serenity.

So today I am 54 years young, no longer the pretty blond girl with the long wavy hair but gray and with all the signs of aging, including aches and pains of body and heart. It is not easy being part of the "Sandwich Generation," squeezed tightly in between children on the one hand, as well as old and failing parents and in-laws on the other. However, for one day I will leave it all, out here in the countryside of New Jersey, and return to my old New York City roots.

photo by Eric Perreault!

Approaching the City from the New Jersey side and taking in the fascinating skyline, I feel my heart beating faster as it always does. Once emerging from the Lincoln Tunnel I open the car window and breathe in deeply the familiar never changing smell of this great city. No longer does it fill me with the wonder it once did. Not any more, for we have carried on a long-term love affair and are extremely comfortable with each other. Easily I feel myself becoming part of what to me seems like a huge pulsating heart of stone and cement, yet vibrantly alive and beating with the energy of a million dreams. Dreams which keep coming from all corners of the world, dreamt by members of every race, color and religion.

Ultimately it all combines into one huge life-force brimming with such energy, such electricity, that I can sense it physically. Our first stop is a familiar parking area near Canal Street, the heart of Chinatown. This is where I wanted to begin today's journey through the day. Not in the upscale area uptown, which I am equally familiar and comfortable with, but here, the center of the old part that is New York, where dreams keep coming ashore and new realities are daily being born. These are the real New Yorkers, the ones who still struggle, the ones who work so very hard to fulfill the dreams, generation after generation. They come from different areas of our world all in the pursuit of the very same dream.

By the time we have made our way to our favorite restaurant, our stride picking up automatically because otherwise we feel out of sync, I have looked into faces so different from mine and from each other, yet all with the same longing I felt when I first came. Freedom and the pursuit of a happy life, unlimited opportunity irregardless of family status; so very different from the other worlds we all chose to leave behind.

While ordering our favorite Szechuan meals we listen to the calming Chinese music in the background and the soft conversation of the other diners. A lot of Asians but also South Americans, Europeans and yes, I distinctly hear the guttural German language spoken in some corner of the establishment. All the sounds intermingle, and I ask myself as I always do when in this big heart of New York, why it is that this wonderful experiment of human beings coming together from all over has not yet taken hold in the rest of the world? Why does the strife and warfare over different races, colors, religions and philosophies have to continue and inflict the pain I know so well over and over and over? Why can't we just allow each other to simply BE, without inflicting hurt on our fellow man?

I don't see color, nor do I see race, religion or anything else but the individual, just the person and I try to catch a glimpse of their heart . Taken as such and mixed up with all the others, I love the resulting flavor of humanity.

The food is delicious, the flavors so very pungent and distinctive, foreign to the German palate I grew up with. However, even my parents liked it here many years ago. By then their minds had broadened a little and I remember them both feeling the energy of New York City. As a matter of fact, I am still astounded that, without being able to speak any English, they would still venture into the City all by themselves in their 60s and early 70s. Once there, they would explore and always make it back home safely, then excitedly tell us about all the sights they had seen. Those were most likely the happiest times they ever had together. New York captured their hearts as it did mine, and to this day my mother, with eyes that no longer see, visits the sights of New York City in her mind that were so dear to her.

I remember once they returned from one of their outings with a really kitschy replica of the Statue of Liberty. It was precious to them and crowned their TV for many years. Now it stands near my mother's bed in the nursing home. I know because I have seen it there. As I mentioned before, I do not see a single picture or reminder of my father, nor does she ever mention him, but that is between her, her God and my father's spirit. It is off-limits to me, I have come to accept that too.

After our meal we reenter the narrow streets of Chinatown, step into a Chinese bakery for some special treats and make our way to PEARL Paint on Canal Street, where upon entering I feel as though I am standing on hallowed ground. We need some art supplies for my son's pen and ink drawings and my husband's photography. This leaves me time to just look around the old store and wonder whose famous artist's feet have touched the ancient worn-out floors and whose hands have held onto the railings leading from one floor to another. I am sure if I knew, I would be in total awe. The people here are wonderfully earthy and eccentric. They shop here because they are true artists or teachers of art, not only because it has to offer just about everything an artist of the visual arts could want, but because it is PEARL'S! They don't want gleaming sterile shelves to pick from. They don't care about the ancient discolored floorboards or the banisters with layer upon layer of old paint. This is an experience in itself, a moment to be savored, because other than the artists picking out the instruments or materials for their art, everything else blends into the background unless, like me right now, I take in the entire picture.

Having found what he was looking for, my husband pays and we head back to the car into the madness of New York City traffic, not for the faint of heart. We make our way past Trinity Church and Wall Street, where a young couple is unsuccessfully trying to take a picture of their young children on the back of the statue of the Bull. Downtown has changed a great deal since 1969, especially the skyline, but the ambiance is still the same. While the old home for the Merchant Marines is being dwarfed by an adjacent skyscraper, it is still there and we make our way to the Staten Island Ferry which, to our great surprise, is FREE now. What a deal! It is the only thing I ever knew to decrease in price, never mind that a nickel was not a fantastic bargain to begin with.

We wait in the big hall watching the pigeons scamper about for food. They are street-wise and know who is a

239

"soft touch." I look around and again see faces from all over the world, peacefully coexisting with each other while waiting patiently.

Once we board and pull out on this beautifully sunny day, the skyline of Manhattan is as glorious as ever, and my husband gets misty-eyed when passing Governor's Island, where he spent a lot of time when being in the Coast Guard before we met. He was lucky not having to go to Vietnam, and he enjoyed his service in the Coast Guard. I look over at Brooklyn and know that somewhere I have distant relatives there whom I have never met.

They owned a German bakery at one time. I believe it was a sister of my maternal grandfather who immigrated and stayed. Next time I'll have to look at the names on the wall where all the immigrants landing on Ellis Island are engraved. The Verrazano Bridge stretches out in front of us and many tankers are pulling in that day, empty container vessels, riding high on the water. Once on Staten Island we have to get off the boat, enter a different terminal and wait a few minutes to catch the ferry back to Manhattan. This time we stand on the bow, facing the wind and passing the Statue of Liberty.

I suddenly feel my father's presence very strongly. To him, although staunch German that he was, the Statue of Liberty stood for freedom and all the opportunities he was denied in his youth. He should have come. He should have been a little more like me, adventurous and standing up to his mother. Why did he not refuse to get married to a woman he did not love and instead follow his dream to become a painter? I know he would have made it but apparently he could not jump over his own shadow. Beaten down by a father who was a drunkard and a cruel man, his ambitions and talents were squashed. I can truly feel his presence and the longing of an unfulfilled dream to follow the road less traveled. Since he believed that one lives on in one's children, it is up to me to carry out his artistic ambition; what if it is in a different medium, does it matter?

All of a sudden I hear a saxophone playing downstairs. It is a lovely sound and I steal away for a minute to be closer, put a dollar in the old man's case and whisper a special "thank you for my birthday song" into his ear. He absolutely beams at me and plays even better than before. I hope he knows how much his play enhanced an already perfect day. Back in Manhattan I express the wish to walk over to the Hope Garden, it being June, the month of roses, I can see it already from a distance. A huge mass of full, shockingly pink roses, planted by loving hands in memory of the victims of HIV and AIDS. We sit on a park bench and people-watch for a while, which turns into bird watching, since just a few yards away a small drama is being played out. A tiny sparrow and a pigeon are both laying claim to a crust of bread and while the pigeon is 10 times the size of the sparrow, the little guy has guts and finally wins the battle. A David and Goliath scenario just played itself out. "Goes to show you," I say to my spouse, "its not the size that counts but the persistence and the courage." That sparrow is a true risk-taker and survivor. Lifting my eyes from the pavement and giving my full attention to the people around, it comes to me that we are all risk-takers and survivors. Especially the first generation of immigrants who come here. My Chinese friends Xuhong and Quizan come to mind, now Annie and Jack, who find themselves still standing with one leg in the cultural traditions of the East but have become American citizens, and the other leg is firmly implanted in the American soil. They have achieved a lot for a young couple. After only ten

241

years and through hard work they now own a nice house, nice cars and both have good, well-paying jobs plus a new baby son. He will belong to this culture entirely. I truly hope his parents will allow him that and not "bind his feet" with rules that don't apply here. It will be a shock to them when he grows up, that much I know already.

However, judging from observing my own sons and from others in my situation, I also know that the second generation does not seem to have the drive of their parents nor the risk-taking ability. Maybe that is the required prerequisite for coming here.

We decide that it is time to retrieve our car from the parking garage where we left it and start heading home. I really don't want this day to end, but I have taken every moment of my 54th birthday outing and enjoyed it to the fullest. Now in my fifties I feel myself getting restless again. There is so much out there I have not seen, have not explored. So much to do, so many friends as yet unmet, that the Tumbleweed part of me is on the move again.

And I wonder where the wind will take me in the years to come. I am ready for new experiences and interesting places. My children do not understand, my husband to a degree, but I know now that I will not set myself boundaries and that I must follow the wind wherever it takes me. For a Tumbleweed it is the right thing to do. It brought me to these shores where I was able to fulfill myself and only God knows where the wind will take me next. It will be a worthwhile journey, for both my husband and myself, of that I am sure.

And so I hope that you, the reader, will wish me a good journey and take away some positive thoughts from this book, the most important one I hope is not to judge a people and punish them in their entirety for things that happened in the past and they had no control over. If there is nothing else you take away, that in itself will be a benefit to mankind.

THE END

Postscript:

The last chapter was written prior to the horrible events which took place on September 11, 2001; to be exact on June 8, 2001. When confronted with the images of the tragedy unfolding in front of me on the television screen I was forced to leave the room on numerous occasions feeling extreme anxiety. It just confirmed to me the fact that mankind is deeply flawed but I simply cannot give up hope that some day, somehow, we will all come to accept and respect each other for who we are, losing the desire to dominate or hurt one another. Without that hope deep in my heart, naïve as it may be, what is the sense living in this world, trying to do and be the best we are capable of? It is the hope that keeps us motivated to reach for the best in us and frankly, if we fail, I truly believe mankind is doomed.

I could not sleep the night following September 11, 2001. In my mind I revisited the destruction of my hometown of Cologne, finding myself walking as a child through piles of rubble. The next morning I received phone calls from a few German girlfriends, and all of them asked me the same identical questions: "Were you able to sleep last night? Where were you in your mind?" All of them had experienced the same feelings of anxiety, whether they saw themselves in Leipzig, Essen or Hamburg, surviving bombs dropping from the sky or walking through vast fields of utter destruction. The most difficult question came last: "Inge, do you think we will ever be able to forget?" "I am afraid not," I answered, "we were just children and carry our scares deep inside ourselves where they are not visible to others." After all, we have never been able to talk about them!

However, listening to my friends, I could not detect hate, prejudice or condemnation, only sadness at the human condition and anger towards the actual perpetrators of this crime, because our country of choice had been violated. I was happy to hear nothing but compassion for the victims and survivors as well as those, who undoubtedly would find themselves in the same position we experienced in our childhood during the months or years to come: the innocent civilians.

WE LEARNED THROUGH EXPERIENCE AND WE LOVE THIS COUNTRY DEEPLY. GIVEN THE FACT THAT HUMANKIND IS FLAWED UNIVERSALLY, AT LEAST HERE WE ARE ABLE TO EXPRESS OUR THOUGHTS AND FEELINGS FREELY WITHOUT FEAR OF REPRISAL.

Inge Perreault

ABOUT THE AUTHOR

Inge Perreault is a writer who shows great diversity in her work. Poetry or prose, short stories based on fact or fiction, newspaper commentaries with a keen sense of humor and social criticism, in all her writing an intense passion for the relevant subjects find expression.

She has written for various national publications, periodicals and newspapers, leading to the publishing of her first book *Duck Soup – Vignettes of Country Life*. Encouraged by the response from readers she chose to demonstrate her diversity in releasing *Birth of a Tumbleweed*. Almost two years in the making, this book shows a side of her life few people are familiar with. The author embarks on the painful journey back into her childhood, growing up amidst the rubble and destruction after the Second World War in her country of birth, Germany. While she emerges from the experience deeply scarred, the title of the book shows us the face of a true survivor. Through sheer determination and persistence she overcomes one hurdle after another; never forgetting where she comes from and what she learned about the human condition.

Since this is a very personal disclosure of her experiences, Inge Perreault has chosen to act as her own editor, in the attempt to be as truthful and authentic as possible. While the actual Tumbleweed breaks off and is blown about by the wind, doing so it leaves behind precious seeds. It is the author's greatest hope that she too leaves behind in her work "seeds" for better understanding, tolerance and acceptance of each other. This book is especially relevant after the events on September 11, 2001.

Inge Perreault lives in New Jersey with her husband Roland Perreault. She raised two sons, Marc and Eric Perreault whom she considers to be her greatest accomplishments.